MARKETING FOR THERAPISTS

WITHDRAWN

The Jossey-Bass Managed Behavioral Healthcare Library
Michael A. Freeman, General Editor

NOW AVAILABLE

Marketing for Therapists: A Handbook for Success in Managed Care
Jeri Davis, Editor

The Computerization of Behavioral Healthcare: How to Enhance Clinical Practice, Management, and Communications
Tom Trabin, Editor

Behavioral Risk Management: How to Avoid Preventable Losses from Mental Health Problems at Work
Rudy M. Yandrick

The Complete Capitation Handbook
Gayle L. Zieman, Editor

Inside Outcomes: The National Review of Behavioral Healthcare Outcomes
Tom Trabin, Michael A. Freeman, and Michael Pallak

Managed Behavioral Healthcare: History, Models, Strategic Challenges, and Future Course
Tom Trabin and Michael A. Freeman

Behavioral Group Practice Performance Characteristics: The Council of Group Practices Benchmarking Study
Allen Daniels, Teresa Kramer, and Nalini Mahesh

How to Respond to Managed Behavioral Healthcare: A Workbook Guide for Your Organization
Barbara Mauer, Dale Jarvis, Richard Mockler, and Tom Trabin

FORTHCOMING

Forming and Managing a Group Practice
Stuart J. Ghertner and Ronald B. Hersch, Editors

Legal and Ethical Challenges in Managed Behavioral Healthcare
John Petrila, Editor

MARKETING FOR THERAPISTS

A Handbook for Success in Managed Care

A VOLUME IN THE JOSSEY-BASS
MANAGED BEHAVIORAL HEALTHCARE LIBRARY

Jeri Davis, EDITOR

Foreword by Michael A. Freeman,
GENERAL EDITOR

Jossey-Bass Publishers
San Francisco

A volume in the Jossey-Bass Managed Behavioral Healthcare Library.

Substantial discounts on bulk quantities of Jossey-Bass books are available to corporations, professional associations, and other organizations. For details and discount information, contact the special sales department at Jossey-Bass Inc., Publishers (415) 433–1740; Fax (800) 605–2665.

For sales outside the United States, please contact your local Simon & Schuster International Office.

 Manufactured in the United States of America on Lyons Falls Pathfinder Tradebook. This paper is acid-free and 100 percent totally chlorine-free.

Library of Congress Cataloging-in-Publication Data

Marketing for therapists: a handbook for success in managed care/
 Jeri Davis.
        p. cm.—(A volume in the Jossey-Bass managed behavioral
 healthcare library)
    Includes bibliographical references and index.
    IBSN 0–7879–0207–1 (alk. paper)
    1. Psychotherapy—Practice—United States. 2. Managed mental
 health care—United States. 3. Psychotherapy—United States—
 Marketing. I. Davis, Jeri, date–. II. Series: Jossey-Bass
 managed behavioral healthcare library.
 RC465.6.M37   1996
 616.89'14'068—dc20
                                                                95–44177
                                                                CIP

FIRST EDITION
PB Printing 10 9 8 7 6 5 4 3 2 1

CONTENTS

FOREWORD

Behavioral healthcare has changed. The old and familiar professional landscape now seems disorienting and altered. The familiar landmarks that were well known to mental health administrators, clinicians, insurance executives, EAP directors, and academic researchers are fading off the map. Vanishing or gone are the employers who didn't pay attention to healthcare costs, the insurance plans that would reimburse on a fee-for-service basis, the hospitals with beds filled by patients with coverage encouraging long lengths of stay, the solo clinicians with full practices of affluent patients seeking long-term insight-oriented therapy, and the community mental health centers that worked in a system of their own.

The scenery of today is different. Health maintenance organizations and managed behavioral health plans have replaced the insurance companies. Employers and purchasing cooperatives are bypassing even these new organizations and purchasing directly from providers. Clinicians are forming group practices. Groups are affiliating with facilities. Facilities are forming integrated delivery systems. Integrated delivery systems are building organized systems of care that include HMOs, care management, and sophisticated management information systems. These information systems are linking payers, managers, and providers into coordinated and comprehensive systems with new levels of accountability. The boundaries of the public sector are eroding, and the distinction between public and private has become more difficult to perceive.

Methods

How can we operationalize the new paradigms, the new models and systems of care needed to make the promise of managed care come true? New methods of benefit administration and health services delivery will be required to implement this vision within realistic financial limits.

At the broadest level, these methods include the core technologies used to manage benefits, care, and the health status of individuals and defined populations. At the level of frontline operations, these methods include continuous quality improvement, process reengineering, outcomes management, public-private integration, computerization, and delivery system reconfiguration in the context of capitation financing. These are the skill sets that The Managed Behavioral Healthcare Library helps you build through an ongoing series of pragmatic professional publications.

New methods of direct clinical care are also required. Instead of treating episodes of illness, disease-state management methods will allow clinicians in future managed and integrated behavioral healthcare systems to reduce morbidity and mortality for individuals and for groups. The Managed Behavioral Healthcare Library also provides frontline clinicians and delivery system managers with the skills that enable our healthcare systems to truly provide scientifically validated bio-psycho-social treatment of choice in behavioral healthcare.

Adjusting to this "brave new world" is challenging enough, and many mental health professionals are tempted to give up and opt out now. But for most of us the challenge is worth facing. While this period is fraught with difficulty and risk, there are a number of opportunities. Whenever a paradigm shifts, those having a stake in the previous paradigm risk losing their place in the one that emerges. In a nutshell, the Managed Behavioral Healthcare Library will help you identify and confront the challenges you will face as the prevailing healthcare paradigms change. Moreover, the volumes in this series will provide you with pragmatic strategies and solutions you can call upon to sustain your importance in the healthcare systems of the future.

In spite of the upheavals transforming the behavioral healthcare enterprise, many basic goals remain the same. In fact, managed behavioral healthcare has come about largely because our previous way of doing things failed to solve fundamental problems related to the cost, quality, access, and outcomes of care. The promise of "managed behavioral healthcare"—whatever this concept may eventually come to mean—holds out the hope of affordable, appropriate, and effective mental health and addiction treatment services for all. The various initiatives and efforts that are under way to reach this new plateau will result in a vast array of professional opportunities for the behavioral healthcare specialists whose talents are required to make this promise come true.

By reading the books and reports in the Managed Behavioral Healthcare Library, you will learn how to respond to the perils and possibilities presented by the shift to managed behavioral healthcare. The authors of this book and other volumes in this series recognize the need for direct and pragmatic solutions to the challenges posed by the new landscape that is becoming the home for our efforts.

To help readers obtain the resources and solutions required, each chapter of each publication is written by an outstanding expert who can communicate in a pragmatic style to help you make a difference. In this way, The Managed Behavioral Healthcare Library provides resources to help readers meet each of the key challenges posed by the new landscape in behavioral healthcare. This volume and the others planned for the series help you improve your effectiveness at pricing, financing, and delivering high-quality, cost-effective care. Future volumes will provide straightforward solutions to the ethical challenges of managed behavioral healthcare and offer advice about practice management and marketing during a period of industry consolidation.

You can look forward to still other books and reports about developing and managing a group practice, creating workplace-based behavioral healthcare programs, measuring outcomes, computerizing delivery systems, and other ways of "benchmarking" and comparing your own organization or practice with others that face similar challenges.

Since the landscape of behavioral healthcare is in flux, professionals in the field need to be aware of alternative future scenarios that might emerge, and develop the skill sets for success within each one. For behavioral healthcare leaders, it is critical to have the vision to select the best options that accord with shared values, and the skills to put these possibilities into practice. For this reason, the themes of vision, action, and results are incorporated into the volumes you read in the Managed Behavioral Healthcare Library.

Vision

In the context of the current debate and upheavals in healthcare, we have seen broad agreement regarding the importance of behavioral health delivery for all Americans, at an affordable price. The Managed Behavioral Healthcare Library offers publications that show how universal coverage for affordable, appropriate, accessible, and effective mental health and addiction treatment benefits and services can be achieved.

Action and Results

Knowing that we are in a period of change, and even having the desire to make the changes that are needed, makes little difference without actions based on methods that can produce results. Since you and the readers of this library take action and produce results through day-in, day-out application of your professional expertise, The Managed Behavioral Healthcare Library is action-oriented to provide the greatest possible benefit to you and your colleagues.

◆ ◆ ◆

Marketing and business development are very new concerns for most behavioral healthcare providers. In fact, many therapists have a distinct aversion to the subject. It must be overcome if one is to survive and prosper in the business of psychology today. *Marketing for Therapists* was written in response to the critical need for this kind of expertise among individual clinicians, group practices, and behavioral healthcare programs and facilities.

Given the consolidation and contraction in the provider environment, simply staying in business has become a pressing real-world concern among providers throughout the country. This volume helps you respond to the rapidly changing and challenging marketplace by providing both fundamental knowledge for the newcomer on practice development systems as well as more sophisticated approaches to marketing for advanced behavioral healthcare groups and programs. The authors are executives, consultants, and seasoned practitioners, whose accumulated experience and insight provide step-by-step guidelines for success.

We hope this book, along with the other volumes in The Managed Behavioral Healthcare Library, provides the information and inspiration essential for all professionals who want to understand the challenges and opportunities available today.

January 1996

Michael A. Freeman, M.D.
Tiburon, California

PREFACE

This book is written for clinicians who work in all areas of mental health and who have responsibility for marketing a behavioral healthcare delivery system. You may be an independent practitioner, or you may be part of a group practice, preferred provider organization, community mental health center, EAP, or other type of behavioral healthcare integrated delivery system. Perhaps, because of your natural skills, you have recently been given a marketing or business development title. Whatever the case, you have a need for a greater understanding of marketing, particularly in the context of the current managed care arena. That is what this book is about.

Marketing for Therapists provides you with practical, usable how-to's for the basic areas of marketing. Much of this book is made up of examples of marketing pieces you can use directly or modify to your situation (the forms in the Appendix are meant to be photocopied for your use). We hope you will keep this book as a handy reference guide, use it often, and copy the forms from it.

Good luck! Remember that much of marketing is common sense filtered through experience. Our goal is to provide you with the best of our practical knowledge. Add your own perspectives and common sense when implementing this information—and have fun with it, because marketing is truly an applied psychology!

Acknowledgments

This book would not exist without the foresight and brilliance of Michael A. Freeman, M.D., president of the Institute for Behavioral Healthcare and editor-in-chief of *Behavioral Healthcare Tomorrow Journal*. May you always be a beacon to those of us navigating the stormy seas of change.

Each of the authors took a deep breath and dove into writing a chapter which synthesized his or her years of knowledge and experience. All of the chapter authors faced significant challenges in translating a tremendous amount of very complicated information into a user-friendly format. The results demonstrate a professional commitment and level of excellence reflective of their professional stature.

One individual read this manuscript even more than I and put in countless hours guiding the direction of this book while it was a work in progress. Our editor at Jossey-Bass, Alan Rinzler, provided invaluable support in a number of areas. He made organizing the entire project understandable and manageable. As a clinician himself, he could review the chapters through the eyes of future readers. And as a professional editor, his sharp pen and critical eye shaped the book into a focused and worthy document. I hope he shares in the professional satisfaction I feel in creating a useful tool for fellow practitioners.

Sandi Millison provided excellent editorial assistance in the chapters I authored. Her sense of humor, intelligence, and calm demeanor were also essential ingredients for surviving some of the more stressful periods of this book editing process.

Lastly, Brian Rubin input and edited, and re-input and re-edited many times over, both my own chapters and others'. His unerring eye for detail and unfailing dedication are traits I admire greatly.

Thank you all for creating this book with me.

January 1996

Jeri Davis
Silver Spring, Maryland

Over the last six years, since starting my marketing firm, three people have been by my side through it all. I would like to acknowledge their invaluable contributions to both my work and my life.

They are my husband, my love, Brian Rubin; my sister, my best friend, Sandi Millison; and my mother, my guide, Frieda Davis. Although your names are not included on the cover of this book, I hope you know that this is as much your book as it is mine.

MARKETING FOR THERAPISTS

CHAPTER ONE

A THERAPIST'S VIEW OF MARKETING

Jeri Davis

Fifteen years ago I sat in my first marketing course, part of the MBA program in which I was newly enrolled. Simultaneously I was taking Ph.D. courses in clinical psychology.

I had no concept of what marketing was. In fact, I thought it was something akin to what you did in a grocery store with a shopping cart. You can imagine my shock and amazement when the professor began the introductory lecture with a description of basic psychology. He explained that marketing is based upon understanding people's needs and motivations, and that marketing is the process of developing services to meet customers' needs at a profit.

I couldn't believe it! Meeting people's emotional needs was why I was interested in becoming a clinician. Here was a professor in the business school teaching a whole new type of applied psychology! So began my fascination and passion for marketing.

With my combined background in psychology and business, I became very interested in marketing psychiatric and substance abuse services because I saw so much stigma against psychiatric care. I set a personal objective to help American consumers overcome some of this stigma, by educating them about when to use such services appropriately.

In addition to the stigma, another major hurdle I found in helping consumers utilize psychiatric services was clinicians' lack of understanding and acceptance of marketing. Over the last fifteen years I have trained hundreds of clinicians in

1

marketing. What I have come up against is not only unjustified prejudice against psychiatric care, but an equal amount of reluctance about marketing on the part of clinical practitioners. Clinicians seem to have a general image of anyone who does marketing as somewhere between a used-car salesman and an outright liar. They frequently see marketing as something they certainly wouldn't want to do themselves. "We are ethical," they seem to think, "and we wouldn't want to push anybody into anything."

The reality is that most good clinicians engage in marketing every day. Gathering background information about clients is a type of marketing research. When you, as a clinician, develop a treatment plan to solve a client's problem, the process is like developing a marketing plan to solve a business problem. And when you convince a client to stick with treatment, take a risk, or follow an aftercare plan, you are selling. Whether your style is consultative, suggestive, or confrontational, the action is the same: you are marketing.

What Marketing Is and Why Most Clinicians Intuitively Know How to Do It

The fundamentals of marketing are based on theories from both psychology and economics. Therefore you will very quickly understand and relate to marketing concepts because most are grounded in human motivation.

Basically, marketing is the psychology of purchase decisions. The process of marketing is determining what services people need or want by doing marketing research, and then developing programs and services to meet these needs. Marketing then goes on to create sales goals and a plan to let people know you have these services (your marketing plan), and finally it monitors to see how things are working (managing your plan).

Additionally, much of marketing implementation relies on common sense and experience. Therefore as you read the examples in this book, relate them to your own experiences and you'll see how much more marketing know-how you possess than you were aware of.

The Ten P's of Marketing

Let's get started with some basic marketing definitions. In a basic marketing course, one of the first things you are taught is that almost all marketing activities are composed of four elements: product, price, place, and promotion. Over the years I have found these terms insufficient in defining the particular scope of behavioral healthcare marketing. So a few years ago I sat down and wrote the Ten P's of Marketing, to incorporate all the marketing activities you will ever engage in:

1. People
2. Products
3. Price
4. Planning
5. Place
6. Promotion
7. Positioning
8. Packaging
9. Producing
10. Pleasing

When I train clinicians, I use the Ten P's to begin to create a common marketing language or terminology. I find that people often use the word *marketing* when they really mean sales. Other individuals think that all marketing is advertising. Many people, including some who actually work in the marketing field, forget key basics, such as planning or place, when they implement marketing activities. Consequently, when I train I encourage even advanced marketers to use the Ten P's as a checklist to ensure they have not overlooked any of these ten key elements in their marketing plans.

This book is organized with the Ten P's in mind. As I describe each basic component of marketing, I tell you which chapter to refer to for a more detailed presentation of the subject.

People

All marketing starts and ends with meeting customers' needs. If you don't offer a product or a service people need, you simply won't have any customers. If customers aren't satisfied after using your services, they will go elsewhere. Therefore the first step of any marketing effort is to carefully define your customers, in terms of

Who they are

What their needs are

What they are looking to buy

What their purchasing cycle is for services such as yours

What they are willing to pay for your services

Failing to define your customers may result in wasting thousands of dollars in time, money, and lost opportunity. Let me give you an example. Several years ago I did some consulting work for a very large group practice. They did not select any target markets; everyone was a potential customer. They based their "business planning" on whatever potentially lucrative request for service came in by phone or by mail.

The company received a request for an Employee Assistance Program (EAP) service proposal. The CEO told the group, "We certainly know how to provide EAP services; let's respond to the request." In addition, this same CEO had a colleague who was a specialist in posttraumatic stress disorders. The CEO decided to bring him onboard half-time to sell these services to businesses. The decision was made without any research, formal or informal, as to whether such a service was one businesses would buy, or even if this was the best target market for this service!

The same group practice was also growing its child-and-adolescent crisis-intervention services, as well as being in the midst of launching a psychiatric nursing home service. All of this went on while they were operating sixteen outpatient offices, most of which were poorly staffed and poorly managed. By far the bulk of the group's revenue was generated from the testing and counseling provided to inpatient psychiatric patients.

Needless to say, the group wasted thousands of dollars and countless hours heading off in too many directions. They did not have well-thought-through marketing goals and target markets. Worst of all, they were so focused on all the new opportunities that they forgot to pay attention to their major customers' (insurance payers) needs. Hence, when managed care arrived, they were unprepared for the crippling financial losses of having their inpatient business cut in half.

Thoroughly researching your prospective customers and their purchasing preferences is time consuming and expensive. Individuals in a hurry to market a new service, or operating on a tight budget, often cut this critical step short. As you see, the results of this oversight can be disastrous.

An example with a more positive ending was a clinician who had a special talent for treating families. She recognized that this strength could be applied to helping individuals struggling in family-run businesses. By researching the needs of this group and formulating specialized services to meet family-owned businesses' mental health needs, she developed this niche and became nationally known for her successful techniques.

Chapter Two, "Responding to the Changing Behavioral Healthcare Marketplace," provides an overview of the marketplace pressures and trends that are changing what customers want and will pay for. It also reviews a variety of alternatives for responding to these trends, factors to consider in choosing your response, and how to approach the important managed care customer.

Chapters Three and Four provide you with information on how to research your target markets and avoid making the classic marketing mistake of not starting with the customer first. Chapter Three, "Target Marketing," presents the key customer groups who make purchase decisions in a managed care environment. The chapter also provides you with examples of how to find the decision makers within managed-care organizations (MCOs)—who control and manage healthcare costs and utilization—and how to derive business from them.

Products

Products are the services you provide based on customer demand. As behavioral healthcare providers, we offer customers a wide array of services, such as individual, marriage, and family counseling; medications management; psychoeducational groups; crisis intervention; and case management.

I use the words *products* and *services* interchangeably for several reasons. First, all the basic principles used to market products can be applied to marketing services. Second, all the primary tools of marketing—advertising, direct mail, sales, workshops, and so on—can be used equally effectively for selling products as well as services. Finally, in the healthcare industry today, whenever we are selling actual products, such as medical equipment or software, we are often simultaneously selling (and people are really buying) the service aspects of the product, such as a twenty-four-hour support line or repair services. Hence, in today's highly technical and service-oriented economy, products and services are intertwined. For example, in the near future, insurance products—such as HMOs and preferred provider organizations (PPOs)—will be sold by healthcare delivery systems—such as hospitals and provider groups.

The most forward-thinking behavioral healthcare marketers are beginning to include value-added products or services in their service arrays. Value-added services are additional features and benefits provided to payers or users at no extra cost. Value-added services for clients include an extra-long first session, free phone support, or free follow-up interviews. For MCOs, online communications (paperless records) and staff with outstanding credentials in a wide variety of specialties would be considered value-added services.

An excellent example is Michele Deveraux, a very progressive vice president of marketing for an HMO, who negotiated value-added services for her traditional HMO plan. These value-added services made the plan far more attractive to singles and families with young children. Deveraux went to local day care centers and spas in her downtown service area and negotiated exclusive discount rates for the HMO members. Should we consider these financial savings to end users products or services? I'm not sure it matters. But I am sure that this savvy marketer dramatically increased customers' satisfaction and retention by building in these nontraditional, customer-valued benefits.

In Chapter Four, "Deciding What Services to Provide," we focus on product development, showing you how to market-test new products. In that chapter you also learn the key steps to launching a new service based on researching customer needs.

Price

Price is what the market will pay for the services you offer. Many individuals mistakenly think that the way to determine the price of a service is to calculate cost and then add a percentage for profit. Although this is how many people set prices to produce profit, it is not the best way to *maximize sales*. Rather, prices are best set by researching what your target audiences are willing to pay.

If there is an oversupply of services similar to those you provide, purchasers will pay less and promote highly competitive bidding processes to bring prices down as low as possible. Conversely, if you are the only provider of a service in high demand, buyers will pay a premium.

You may think your organization's services are exceptional, but if you have five or more direct competitors in your immediate geographic service area then don't expect managed care purchasers to pay any more for your services than they are paying other providers. On the other hand, if yours is the only organization in your area offering home-based crisis care, or psychiatric foster home services, don't price these products for managed care organizations at the rate the government was paying you (assuming that government was your major customer previously). Research what MCOs are currently using as an alternative to your service and what they're paying for it, and establish your pricing with this as a starting point.

The primary driving forces behind managed care are cost cutting and cost control. The number one goal of purchasers of all types is to cut costs while maintaining acceptable quality of healthcare. Therefore managing your costs very closely and developing a keen understanding of how to price your services is of critical importance.

In a price-driven environment, you can only compete so far on price before profit margins are cut to the bare minimum. According to behavioral healthcare industry watchers, pricing today is so competitive that there is at best a 15 percent range of variation in what managed care companies will pay different providers for a given product or service. The best way to obtain the highest price within a competitive range is to prove that you can offer end users and purchasers something more that they are willing to pay for. These value-added services distinguish your organization from competing providers.

Chapter Seven, "Managed Care Contracting," teaches you how to fill out contract applications so that you are in a position to receive the best reimbursement possible. We explain different pricing options, such as case rates, capitation, and flat fees. In addition, we present creative bundling of services to help you identify ways to build reimbursement through value-added services.

Planning

Planning is deciding what you will do ahead of time to reach your marketing goals cost-efficiently. Planning includes all of the following steps:

- Researching and prioritizing target markets
- Evaluating market trends and changes
- Comparing your organization to the competition in terms of strengths, weaknesses, opportunities, and threats
- Reviewing sales and business progress to date
- Identifying what marketing efforts worked or didn't work during the past year
- Deciding what new products to launch in the coming year
- Setting both organizational and marketing goals for the coming year
- And most importantly, translating all of the above information into marketing strategies and an implementation plan

Planning is a complex and comprehensive series of activities upon which all marketing decisions are based. The marketing plan in which all this information is formalized and organized is a critical management tool for anyone leading a marketing effort. Without a marketing plan, you are like a ship without a compass: you don't know where you are, you don't know where you are going, and you don't know how far you've come.

I have learned from personal experience that without a well-researched and well-thought-out marketing plan, any organization with significant competition is doomed to fail.

In the behavioral healthcare industry, tight profit margins do not allow using resources inefficiently or making many mistakes. Therefore, it is as important to spend time and resources in the planning phase as it is in the implementation phase. If you have done your homework well, the implementation phase will go much smoother and will be focused only on what you need to do to accomplish specific objectives.

The first part of Chapter Five, "Developing a Marketing Plan and Steps to Successful Sales," walks you through the steps of developing a marketing plan. Following this is a description of the sales process. The author does an excellent job demonstrating the connection between thorough planning and successful sales.

Place

Place, or channels of distribution, refers to where you choose to locate your services. In the managed care arena, *place* is not only used in a geographic sense but also refers to where you will locate your services within a behavioral healthcare delivery system. Many options are available to you. You may choose to become part of a multispecialty group practice; alternatively, you may want to link up with a medical/surgical system or an MCO in order to provide vertically integrated services.

Given the oversupply of behavioral healthcare providers and the rapid industry consolidation currently under way, where you choose to "place" your business is another critical element of survival in a managed care environment.

Chapter Six, "Finding Your Place in the Integrated Delivery System," provides detailed insights regarding the partnering choices available to you. It gives an overview and a definition of the different types of organizations available to link up with, and the pros and cons of each alternative.

Promotion

Promotions are the methods you use to let people know about your products and services. People often confuse promotion and marketing. Promotion encompasses all forms of communicating with customer audiences, such as sales, advertising, publicity, direct mail, professional educational series, community workshops, brochures, posters, testimonials, Yellow Page advertising, etc. The creative ways in which you can communicate with target customer groups are almost limitless.

The key goals for any successful promotion are to build *awareness* and *preference*. This is done through the consistency and repetitiveness of the messages relayed. The steps of promotion are very similar to the steps of a sale. In both cases we use a multimedia approach to build a relationship with prospective buyers. In order to build a relationship, you need to go through the following process:

Step 1:   Build awareness. Educate decision makers about who you are, and establish credibility and trust.

Step 2:   Build product awareness. Educate decision makers about the services you have to offer.

Step 3:   Build product preference. Demonstrate how the services you offer can successfully meet an individual's or an organization's needs.

Step 4:   Create product differentiation. Demonstrate how your services are different from and better than others available in the marketplace.

Step 5:   Identify and respond to objections and concerns.

Step 6:   Close the sale. Ask for the contract or referral.

As you can see from the above steps, the process of building awareness and preference is not necessarily easy. There are many tools available to help you communicate effectively with prospects. Chapter Eight, "Promoting Your Services," provides a lot of concrete advice for implementing successful promotions, including many helpful tips for using publicity, networking, and speaking engagements as well as other methods for building your business.

Positioning

Positioning is the process of creating a unique image or reputation for your organization or yourself in the minds of customers. The power and economic value of positioning cannot be overestimated. In their book *The 22 Immutable Laws of Marketing*, Al Ries and Jack Trout do the best job of quantifying the value of obtaining the number one position in the minds of customers. Ries and Trout demonstrate the concept that mind share equals market share: the market leader tends to have twice the market share or revenue of the brand in second place. Among psychiatric hospital chains in 1994, the market leader, Charter Medical Corporation, had almost three times the net operating revenue ($902 million) as the closest competitor, Community Psychiatric Centers ($322.9 million). Similarly, as outpatient provider groups consolidate and form super groups, a few outpatient leaders will emerge in each market based in part on establishing leadership positions in the minds of both payers and customers.

Further, in the managed healthcare industry, health plans seek out physicians and hospitals with the best reputations. Consumers in turn seek out the health plans with the hospitals and doctors having the best reputations. Similarly, in behavioral health, if you have a good reputation within the provider community, you will be sought out by more managed care panels. Also, if you cultivate top-of-mind awareness and develop a good reputation among case managers and network managers within managed care organizations, you are more likely to get a larger share of referrals than other providers not engaging in this type of effort. In other words, "mind share" is often very closely tied to market share, no matter what industry you are in.

Chapter Eight includes guidelines and strategies for establishing a unique position among your competitors and suggestions for using promotions to build a positive reputation.

Packaging

Packaging is describing and configuring to your services to make them more attractive to target audiences. Packaging is "selling the sizzle," or, as I call it, "buying the box."

Recently, I was helping a provider launch a new outpatient center targeting the geriatric market. To build interest and awareness, the center was offering a series of workshops on "grief and loss." Unfortunately, the response to the center's newspaper advertising was dismal. I pointed out to the client that one reason for the low response rate was their packaging of the workshop. "People don't buy problems, such as grief and loss," I explained. "Most of us have enough problems already without 'buying' more of them." Rather, people buy "hope" and solutions to their problems framed in a positive way. I suggested changing the name of the workshop to "Rebuilding Your Life After a Loss." Running an ad with this new packaging four times in the local newspaper, they tripled the response rate in a month!

In America, every time we go to the grocery store we make many of our purchase decisions based solely on the packaging—the words, the colors, and the written or implied promises. Dry-goods marketers have long subscribed to the power of packaging to influence sales.

Examples of packaging in the behavioral healthcare field are service brochures, responses to proposals, sales presentations, and even office location and environment. Your organization's brochure says more about you than just what is written in the copy. Do you use a solid, quality paper that conveys a message of company stability? Do you have a logo that creates a strong, positive message and differentiates you from competitors? Do the physical surroundings of your office convey comfort, safety, and the promise of a caring, personal experience?

Recently, I conducted a series of focus groups with major employers and asked them what factors would positively or negatively impact their purchasing decision on a managed behavioral healthcare network. One vice president in charge of benefits rejected a candidate simply because there were too many typos in the submitted proposal! If the provider group could not even put together a decent proposal, this executive reasoned, what quality of healthcare could they deliver?

Another member of the focus group said she rejected an organization because the salesperson was disorganized, unprepared, and unprofessional. Although the salesperson had nothing at all to do with the delivery of healthcare services being evaluated for purchase, the prospective customer rejected the company because of the poor presentation—the disorganized packaging—by the salesperson who represented them.

In the managed care environment, packaging can also refer to the bundling of various combinations of services and prices to make services more attractive to purchasers. For example, an all-inclusive price that incorporates physician fees and follow-up care is very attractive to MCOs. Adding value-added services, such as free aftercare groups or free educational classes for managers as part of a package price, will often make one provider more attractive over another and win the sale.

Chapter Seven, "Managed Care Contracting," and Chapter Eight, "Promoting Your Services," touch on different areas of packaging in behavioral healthcare. Chapter Seven talks about package pricing and value-added services. Chapter Eight provides a number of examples on how to package and promote yourself or your network.

Producing

Producing is delivering on your promises. It is providing the services you are in the business to deliver, such as group therapy or twenty-four-hour crisis services. The best way to lose a customer is to fail to deliver on your promises. This is where many organizations get into trouble. They overpromise and underdeliver.

For example, several years ago I worked with a large behavioral healthcare organization that almost contracted itself out of business. The organization's vice president of business development was not at all involved in clinical operations. Not only did he lack involvement, but this individual did not have any formalized communications systems within the organization to gather or relay contracting information. Consequently he negotiated many contracts and promised services at prices the organization could not profitably deliver. Fortunately, the organization was owned by a larger parent company that could carry these losses until it renegotiated contracts that were realistic. Few provider organizations today have the luxury of such a financial cushion. It is essential to set up communication systems, both within a provider network and between a network and its contractees, to ensure that promises are clearly understood and kept.

Chapter Nine, "Customer Service," provides examples of the types of systems which must be put into place to guarantee that products are delivered as promised.

Pleasing

The last two of the Ten P's of marketing, producing and pleasing, go hand in hand. Pleasing refers to servicing and meeting customer needs. Whereas producing is *what* you do, pleasing is *how* you do it. Because of the technical and intangible nature of the services we provide, end users often judge the quality of what we do by how we do it. Secondly, but equally important, good service is inextricably tied to repeat business, renewed contracts, and long-term success.

Servicing and satisfying customers also has additional significance in the behavioral healthcare field. A growing body of research supports the premise that client satisfaction is related to overall measures of outcome, as well as patient compliance with treatment. This means the more satisfied clients are with treatment, the greater the likelihood they will experience better outcomes and complete recommended courses of treatment.

Servicing customers includes all customer groups. In the managed care environment, customers include payers, intermediaries (case managers), referring agents, and end users. You cannot forget to service any customer group without having negative consequences.

Regular and meaningful communication with customers is the key to successful service. Most contracts are lost because of failed communications. Customers may become angry about or dissatisfied with an element of service but not convey their dissatisfaction to the provider until it is too late. This usually happens because the provider does not develop open communication systems with clients and does not regularly seek feedback. As a result, clients show their anger by taking their business elsewhere. This is a great waste of marketing dollars and effort. The least expensive form of marketing is maintaining satisfied customers; the most expensive is generating new accounts and winning satisfied clients from competitors. As more and more markets are divided up into a limited number of big contracts, few organizations will be able to afford poor customer service.

The last chapter of this book, "Customer Service," details the steps necessary for setting up good customer service systems. This will be an area of increasing emphasis in coming years.

How Marketing Has Shifted Under Managed Care

The introduction of managed care, fueled by cost containment and technological advances, has propelled behavioral healthcare into being a mature market. In a mature market, costlier but less efficient products, such as inpatient psychiatric care, are phased out and replaced by new, lower cost alternatives, such as home-based crisis intervention and brief therapy. The profit margins of traditional products are flat and declining, while margins are increasing on innovative products.

Intensive competition forces organizations that are unable to adapt out of business. Survivors compete by establishing market dominance and a unique niche. Most business is done via contracting and sales. Successful players thrive by mastering the sales process, serving customers well, and establishing long-term, mutually beneficial relationships. These winners provide value as well as competitive prices. Their products and services constantly evolve to meet changing customer demands.

Marketing in a mature market is more complex and has greater risks than in a growing market, such as was present in the 1980s. Therefore marketing activities in the 1990s and twenty-first century need to be more sophisticated. Consequently, this complex situation creates obstacles and opportunities for success. If you choose to look on the negative side, your viewpoint might be, "There is a good likelihood that there will be little or no need for my services within the next two to three years." On the other hand, if you choose to look on the positive side, you can begin to see all the new product and business opportunities emerging along with a streamlined behavioral healthcare system.

The next chapter helps you see these opportunities so you can capitalize on them.

Note

P. 9, *Ries and Trout demonstrate the concept that mind share equals market share:* Ries, A., & Trout, J. (1993). *The 22 immutable laws of marketing.* New York: HarperCollins.

CHAPTER TWO

RESPONDING TO THE CHANGING BEHAVIORAL HEALTHCARE MARKETPLACE

Bruce C. Gorman

Managed behavioral healthcare is here to stay. According to *Open Minds,* the managed behavioral healthcare publication, "Of an estimated 185.7 million Americans with health insurance, approximately 59.8 percent or 111 million are enrolled in some type of specialty managed behavioral health program (including Medicare, this 111 million represents 50.1 percent of the insured population)." Many other individuals are enrolled in a physical managed care program with a behavioral healthcare component. Except for a very few behavioral healthcare professionals who will develop a "carriage trade" niche of private-pay patients, behavioral healthcare professionals will need to embrace managed care principles and practices in order to survive and grow. For those willing to accept and embrace change, managed care will provide opportunities. For those who choose to ignore it, their professional destiny will be in others' hands.

In our era of limited and shrinking resources, the alternative to managed care—the significant reduction or elimination of benefits—is far more draconian. Just ask the 25 million Americans who are uninsured. Which health benefit is most likely to wind up on the surgery room floor? Not maternity or medical benefits. It will, of course, be behavioral healthcare.

A radically changing environment confronts the professional lives and livelihood of behavioral healthcare providers. Those who wish to grow, prosper, and provide needed services to individuals must understand, accommodate, and learn to manage this change. In this chapter, I attempt to provide an introduction to the changing scene in behavioral healthcare delivery and financing, describe the range of responses which providers are adopting, and offer tools and suggestions that assist the reader in choosing her best path. However, no information I provide is of any value unless you make the emotional shift to accepting managed care as reality. Denial is the most profound barrier to behavioral healthcare professionals in accommodating change, and in making it work for them. Once this resistance is overcome, the rest is relatively easy, as long as business and marketing fundamentals are followed.

Responding to the Pressures of the Marketplace

Don't blame the managed care companies! They are responding to marketplace demands to produce more for less. Employers, insurance companies, HMOs, and government purchasers are all passing the pressure to cut costs right on down the line to managed care companies, providers, and other intermediaries. The global market and international competition also affect behavioral healthcare providers because employers are seeking to control healthcare benefit costs to be more productive. For increasingly lower premiums, purchasers are demanding and getting more services, better accountability, and outcome measurements.

The competition is fierce, and providers are feeling the impact. However, we are all in this together. Providers, purchasers, and managed care companies must work together to ensure that the highest quality, most accessible and most cost-effective care is delivered within the limits of available resources.

Purchasers are demanding greater—and provable—value for their healthcare benefits dollars. While providers and MCOs are making great strides to share positive outcomes in behavioral healthcare, purchasers remain skeptical. The behavioral healthcare provider must work with managed care companies to ensure that the purchaser, who ultimately controls the purse strings, is a satisfied customer.

Imbalance of Supply and Demand

Most urban and suburban areas have a substantial oversupply of mental health professionals, particularly psychologists, clinical social workers, and master's-level counselors. A major complaint of providers is that once they are selected to be members of provider panels they don't receive referrals. This is because there are not enough referrals to go around, and because MCOs, either formally or informally, tend to use providers who have demonstrated their ability to provide appropriate, necessary, and quality care in a managed-care-oriented fashion.

Some of the behavioral professional associations have responded by advocating and lobbying for "any willing provider" legislation. This would require the managed care company to include any provider who is licensed and meets credentialing requirements to be included in its network. Such a response is counterproductive, however, and does nothing to confront the core problem of an oversupply and geographic concentration of providers.

The successful provider must carefully address these issues and develop long-term business strategies that anticipate and respond to changing marketplace needs. For example, providing services in underserved rural and inner-city locations would address a marketplace need and is more productive than attempting to create artificial demand for services.

Brief, Problem-Focused Therapy

While this is not intended to be a forum for debate about what constitutes the appropriate clinical focus of care, many behavioral healthcare benefits purchasers have sent a message to the marketplace that they are willing to pay only for services that address the resolution of patients' immediate, presenting issues or problems. Without a clinical philosophy that seeks the appropriate level and intensity of care, the purchaser often addresses the issue by limiting benefits and expenditures for behavioral healthcare services. Put simply, while there may be some instances where the patient and provider feel that working toward permanent character change and growth is appropriate, third-party purchasers are rarely willing to pay for it anymore.

Behavioral healthcare providers must decide if they are able to embrace this treatment philosophy and provide services under these circumstances. Otherwise, the provider must either build his or her practice upon private-pay patients or strongly consider a career change.

Managed Care Versus Limited Benefits

Don't confuse these! Providers often confuse managed care with insurance benefit plans that limit behavioral healthcare benefits. A primary reason why behavioral healthcare benefits have been limited in the first place is because purchasers have not been provided with sufficient information to illustrate the value—the return on their investment—for purchasing behavioral healthcare services. Additionally, some purchasers believe that significant abuses and squandering of limited dollar resources have occurred in the provision of behavioral healthcare.

Most purchasers are continuously looking for means to maintain or reduce the costs of their benefit outlay in order to remain competitive. Managed care is a far more appropriate route to services and cost-containment than continued re-duction of behavioral healthcare benefits. However, the behavioral healthcare provider must work with managed care to ensure quality, accountability, and demonstrated value to purchasers. Time and resources expended on managing care might be better devoted to providing needed clinical services. But that depends on providers and managed care companies' working together to provide quality, cost-effective, and solution-oriented services.

Shifts in Reimbursement Strategy

Gone are the days when providers received payment at time of services, or after simply submitting "billed charges" to the insurance company. Reimbursement of behavioral healthcare services is increasingly based upon fee schedules, which in most cases are dictated by the company or purchaser. Reimbursement is also done today by case rates, capitation (payment of amounts per member per month, regardless of the amount of service provided), or related variations. Providers must recognize the advantages and disadvantages of these approaches and adjust their business and marketing strategies accordingly. Chapter Seven of this book defines each of these payment approaches and their implications for your program or practice.

Provider Initiatives and Responses

Providers are responding to changes in the financing and organization of behavioral healthcare delivery in a variety of ways, most of which require involvement in a system of care that is larger than individual providers. Alas, as with the evolution in healthcare practice and in American business in general, it is increasingly difficult to deliver services in a totally independent, sole practice. While some providers may consider this a loss of autonomy, we should recognize that acceptance of third-party reimbursement compromises autonomy in the first place. At any rate, a provider's response to changing marketplace conditions should be part of his or her overall strategic planning process. Here are some of the most effective options.

Integrated Delivery Systems

Several provider organizations are developing relationships with other providers and provider organizations to develop a full continuum of care, from inpatient to outpatient, in their community or region. In some cases, behavioral healthcare is integrated into physical health care. In other cases, the integration is developed exclusively for behavioral healthcare, sometimes referred to as IBHOs (or integrated behavioral healthcare organizations). These integrated delivery systems are intended to provide managed care companies and other purchasers with one-stop shopping within a community or region and thus be attractive to this market.

Behavioral healthcare providers interested in affiliation with these integrated systems should do market research in their communities to determine which organizations may be developing these systems.

Facility-Owned Services

Sharing certain characteristics with integrated delivery systems, some hospitals and other healthcare facilities are purchasing or creating multispecialty and behavioral group practices to attract purchasers by creating a similar continuum of care. Although the behavioral healthcare provider must consider issues of autonomy or independence in determining whether to follow this path, it is a worthwhile direction to consider in the changing behavioral healthcare marketplace. In today's volatile healthcare environment, the provider is not independent of marketplace factors even in managing an independent practice.

Multispecialty Medical Groups

Multispecialty medical groups that include a behavioral healthcare component are becoming prevalent, particularly on the West Coast. These organizations are very attractive to comprehensive managed care companies such as HMOs, which work with them to cover a specific geographic area or community. In some cases, however, the purchasers will work with a managed behavioral care organization to provide the behavioral healthcare and exclude the multispecialty medical group practice from providing these specific services. Learning about the market position and the advantages and disadvantages of joining a multispecialty medical group should be part of the provider's research.

Behavioral Group Practices

Behavioral group practices are similar to multispecialty medical groups but exclusively comprise behavioral healthcare providers. In some cases, the behavioral group practice is made up of similarly credentialed professionals (for example, psychologists), and in other cases it includes multidisciplinary behavioral healthcare practitioners (perhaps psychiatrists, psychologists, and clinical social workers).

When constituted with high-quality, accessible providers, these groups can be very attractive to general purchasers of healthcare benefits, comprehensive managed care companies, specialty managed behavioral care companies, and provider networks. Many providers are considering developing or forming these group practices, particularly in more-mature managed care markets. This should be a strong consideration to explore in the provider's geographic location.

Provider-Based Managed Care Companies

In some cases providers have formed their own managed care companies. Some of the national and regional managed behavioral care leaders are provider-based organizations, where a significant number of the employees are clinicians. While there are certainly obstacles to entry on the national level, some providers are considering creating local or regional managed care companies. An alternative to forming your own MCO is to develop "strategic alliances," that is, formal and informal business relationships with managed care companies and other purchasers that may have systems or capabilities you, the provider, do not have.

Community Mental Health Organizations

Community mental health organizations (CMHOs) are positioning themselves for managed care, particularly in the public-sector delivery systems (that is, Medicaid, Medicare, block grant programs). CMHOs are developing clients in commercial markets as well. Similarly, relationships with community-based organizations, such as those funded by United Way agencies, should also be explored. These organizations share characteristics with behavioral group practices but add several ancillary services (such as case management, intensive outpatient programs, therapeutic group home programs), which some purchasers and managed care companies find attractive. Behavioral healthcare providers should survey the activities of organizations in their community to learn about opportunities. In some cases, CMHOs and other community-based organizations contract for services with group practices and individual providers.

◆ ◆ ◆

It is important to recognize that the aforementioned responses and initiatives are by no means mutually exclusive or all-inclusive. It is most important for the behavioral healthcare provider to recognize the fundamental and significant changes affecting his or her profession, consider the options that best meet his or her goal, and pursue the direction and strategy most appropriate to his or her situation.

Decision-Making Factors for Providers

Given what has been presented here so far, do you want to try it on your own? Managed care and the "commercialization" of behavioral healthcare services are making this more difficult. The provider who wishes to continue in sole, private practice will have to find a very specific niche to be successful. Although operating a sole practice may give the impression of independence, delivering service under contract to a managed care company or other purchaser or providing care for a patient with insurance quickly proves this notion of independence to be illusory.

Behavioral healthcare providers must decide under what structure they wish to provide services. To do this they must conduct a careful personal and business analysis of the options available, and of the costs and benefits in pursuing each course of action. Here are some of the issues to be considered in this all-important analysis.

Resources Available for Practice

While the cost to launch and sustain a behavioral healthcare practice is clearly less than the cost of a primary care practice, the provider must consider the expense of managing a practice and its ability to compete in increasing competition with group practices, facility-owned services, and other group or organizational providers. As the intense pressure to deliver care more efficiently continues to increase, the behavioral healthcare providers will need to determine their resources and how to invest them appropriately.

Limited resources constitute one of the primary reasons for the growth in group and institutional practices. Managed care companies and other purchasers of care will increasingly require assistance in reporting outcomes, fulfilling regulatory requirements, and demonstrating accountability and efficacy of behavioral healthcare services. The expensive systems required to manage and provide this information must be considered in the provider's decision making.

Advantages and Disadvantages of Group- or Facility-Based Practices

As a behavioral healthcare provider, consider whether you can work successfully in a group practice or in a practice associated with a group, hospital, or other facility. An increasing number of providers are pursuing these options, for a variety of reasons. Without a doubt, the growth and prominence of managed care has created—and will continue to create—a variety of group- and facility-based practices to promote efficiency, cost-effectiveness, the ability to measure quality and outcomes, and market positioning. Advantages of working in a group- or facility-based practice include

- Having a vehicle to work directly with clinical colleagues. Case conferences, consultations, and assistance in formulating treatment planning are readily available.
- Limited or no need to be involved in the business, administrative, and marketing aspects of the practice.
- Enhanced ability to receive contracts and referrals. Group- and facility-based practices, particularly those with excellent access, demonstrated quality, and flexibility, are attractive to managed care companies and other purchasers.
- A steady paycheck! For the provider who has expenses or a family to feed, group practices can often ensure a steady income, particularly in larger facility-based practices.
- Access to information and innovation. Group- and facility-based practices often have the economies of scale and resources to invest in the materials and equipment needed to survive and grow, including management information and billing systems, training and staff development, and outcome and satisfaction measures.

Of course, along with advantages in joining a practice, there are also disadvantages:

- In some cases, reduction in independence results from aligning with a group- or facility-based practice. Supervisors and managers need to be dealt with.
- Possible reduction in income. Any organization has administrative overhead and profit margins to maintain, and some revenues must be earmarked for these expenses. Where risk for clinicians decreases, potential rewards also decrease. The behavioral healthcare provider must consider the potential gains and losses for each alternative.
- Sometimes the individual provider and the group may differ on treatment philosophy. In some cases, discussion and mutual education will resolve these differences. In others, this may not be possible. Clearly, comfort with treatment philosophy and practice must be of utmost concern to the behavioral healthcare provider.

Business Strategy

The behavioral healthcare provider must decide upon a business strategy and how it should be executed. Throughout this chapter we have suggested how important supply and demand are in this evolving field. The clinician must come to terms with an extremely competitive business environment, in which supply significantly exceeds demand, financial resources are shrinking, and purchasers are demanding more value. Developing a business strategy should be a formal process and include a detailed implementation plan and budget.

In such strategic development, the behavioral healthcare provider must consider several factors.

Geographic Considerations. Regardless of how healthcare systems are organized, healthcare will be delivered to patients according to geographic accessibility and availability. Behavioral healthcare providers are known for developing practices near where they want to live, not where the marketplace indicates their services are required. This has resulted in a concentration and oversupply of providers in suburban and upscale urban areas, while there is a dearth of services in rural and lower-income urban areas. Providers must consider location and market demand as major factors in determining where to locate their businesses. Providers should consider being willing to specially accommodate marketplace needs and the requests of managed care companies, such as locating a practice for a day or two a week in a different location—perhaps in a physician's office or a health center. Providers should also perform a careful market location analysis to determine the best place to locate or sublocate their practices or simply make services available.

Market Considerations. In determining where and how to practice, the provider should consider the many submarkets in behavioral healthcare. For example, does the professional wish to provide services to private or public-sector clients, or both? Is there a particular specialty or area of interest that the professional wishes to limit her practice to, for example, women's issues, eating disorders, child and adolescent services? What percentage of the practice should be under managed care arrangements? Does the provider wish to work in a group or in a facility-based practice, or should he or she develop informal linkages with other providers? These decisions need to be based on professional and personal preferences; market, financial, and economic considerations must be prominent factors.

Longevity Considerations. Given the changing nature of the behavioral healthcare market, providers must concern themselves with the future growth and survival of their practice and livelihood. While projecting viability is, at best, an art in this quickly changing environment, the provider should make every effort to track the factors that significantly impact his or her professional survival and livelihood.

Income and Financial Considerations. What are the provider's short-term and long-term financial objectives? Is a salary for working in an organization satisfactory? What is the provider's orientation to risk and being an entrepreneur? Is he or she interested in being involved in the business aspects of a practice? What are the costs of doing business in one's own practice (including professional liability insurance, office overhead, business taxes, equipment and supplies, administrative assistance, and marketing costs) that would not need to be considered in a system-based practice? All of these issues need to be carefully thought out and mindfully analyzed.

Product Differentiation and Positioning

To survive and grow in the competitive behavioral healthcare environment, the provider must seek to differentiate and position his or her product from the competition's. Behavioral healthcare providers must be cognizant that they are involved in a competitive business environment and act accordingly. Here are some differentiation and positioning strategies that relate particularly to the managed care market:

- Develop a clinical practice area which may be in short supply in a market where a managed care company requires coverage. For example, many managed care companies have difficulty locating an adequate number of high-quality child and adolescent providers.
- Provide clinical support services, which managed care companies may desire in addition to providing clinical services. For example, the managed care company may need assistance in delivering mobile crisis, on-site evaluation and assessment, and crisis intervention services.
- Develop relationships with the local community, including employers and medical, educational, and social services institutions, to familiarize them with your practice and services. Most managed care companies go out of their way to include providers in their network, referring patients to providers who are known in their community and who have a previous service arrangement with the patients.
- Work with a group of multidisciplinary providers who can provide a managed care company with significant depth and breadth of coverage in a broad geographic area. This will send a message that you are responding to the managed care company's needs for coverage, accessibility, and choice.

Referral Patterns

Behavioral healthcare providers must do a careful analysis of how referrals are handled in their market areas. Depending upon how the delivery system is established, the benefit design of the purchaser, and how the patient accesses the system, managed care often changes traditional referral patterns. The provider can determine and control for referral factors by

- Carefully analyzing and understanding the benefit design of the patient
- Learning how and on what criteria the referral is made by the managed care company
- Learning if one provider can perform both the assessment and the service delivery
- Learning which other providers work in the same geographic area and whether they can provide similar services
- Learning whether the patient's primary care physician is involved in the referral
- Learning whether services are covered in an open or a closed panel (that is, whether or not services are covered if the patient goes to a provider who is not in the network)
- Carefully analyzing and understanding the provider agreement to ensure compliance with all referral requirements
- Understanding the needs of the managed care companies and the care managers to ensure being considered for referral
- Understanding the utilization and use patterns of the patients in the geographical area
- Determining how to attain preferred referral status and business arrangements with managed care companies

Assessment of Value

Behavioral healthcare providers should continuously assess the value of their practice and service in order to evaluate what their most attractive and appropriate business, professional, and personal options may be. The behavioral healthcare market and the changes related to managed care are so turbulent that constant reevaluation is required. For the astute provider, there are significant opportunities inherent in this change; understanding one's business and clinical worth amidst this change is crucial.

Approaches to Managed Care Companies

Probably the most significant concern of behavioral healthcare providers is evident in this common and perfectly appropriate question: "How do I approach managed care companies to ensure that I am selected to be on a network and receive referrals?"

There are usually more behavioral healthcare providers to choose from than the managed care company needs to provide services. Successful providers need to be positioned to receive a reasonable share of referrals from the relationship. Here are some means to that end:

- Research market needs. Where does the managed care company require services? How many "lives" or employees and family members does it cover? What is its approach to building a network and making referrals? What are the behavioral healthcare benefits under its program?
- Research managed care products. Many products are promulgated under the managed care umbrella, all of which impact the provider's business possibilities. For example, how services are delivered under an HMO has dramatically different implications from how referrals are made under an EAP arrangement. Understanding the differences in these products is a key to identifying and meeting the managed care company's needs.
- Learn how to access decision makers. Meet them in conferences. Find out what their customers' needs are. Invite the decision makers to business and professional association events. Attend local business and healthcare functions where they may be in attendance, and work with your professional association to engage them in positive dialogue. (Historically, providers have used these functions to air their concerns and anxieties about managed care and change.) Create opportunities for common concerns to be addressed constructively.
- Be flexible regarding service and location. What services do the managed care companies need, and where do they need them?
- Align yourself with a group, facility, or system. Simply, there's strength in numbers, continuity of care, and comprehensive services. Managed care companies respond to the strategies of provider organizations that meet their business and clinical needs.
- Differentiate your service. What services are in short supply for the companies that solve their business needs? Can you provide these services?

◆ ◆ ◆

The well-prepared behavioral healthcare provider can turn challenge into opportunity with careful analysis, planning, and action consistent with the changes in the industry. First and foremost, the provider must never think that behavioral healthcare is going to go back to the way it was. Managed care in all its various forms is here to stay, and business, career, and professional planning must be accomplished accordingly. Many observers of behavioral healthcare agree that a significant trend in the industry is the swing back to control by provider organizations and systems that embrace and expand upon the principles of managed care. What will prevail for the provider is the combination of providing excellent care with measurable outcomes and a positive approach to change and business.

Note

P. 14, *"Of an estimated"*: Oss, M. E., Winters, C. M., Stair, T., & Mackie, J. J. (1995). Managed behavioral health market share in the United States 1995–1996. *Open Minds*, p. 4. (Available from Open Minds, 4465 Old Harrisburg Road, Gettysburg, PA 17325.)

CHAPTER THREE

TARGET MARKETING

How to Start the Client Flow

Nancy Lucinian

Whether you are the newly appointed director of community outreach for a community mental health organization, the self-identified marketer for a growing group practice or integrated delivery system, or a newly licensed therapist ready to launch your career in private practice, you may be asking yourself, "How do I expand my organization's client base?" For example, Helen, a local clinician, called me to see if I could help her generate business for her new practice. She had recently left a mental health agency to start a private practice with another clinician. They had just signed a three-year lease for two small offices located in a business complex in a good part of town. Her neighbors were a car insurance agent, a seamstress, and a photographer—not traditional referral sources for mental health professionals.

We began to discuss how she was going to generate patients. She said that she planned to bring some patients with her from her old agency, and she was going to send out an "announcement" with her new address and phone number. She also anticipated telling her colleagues that she was starting a group for "women in transition."

My first reaction was thinking to myself: I hope she doesn't have children to feed!

As a former agency employee, she hadn't needed to be on outpatient provider panels for managed care companies in her area. Nor had her practice pattern included following up with the primary care physicians of her clients. She didn't like public speaking, I learned, and she felt that "marketing" was unprofessional. Where could I begin . . . ? She needed a support group!

Whether you are a physician or a clinician, your education probably did not include classes on business development and management. Such classes would have been especially valuable. Unless you're that rare clinician born fortunately with good business sense, you need to educate yourself about building referral relationships with managed care—especially in developing organizations and other client referral sources. This chapter focuses on how to expand and maintain a flow of clients through your program, practice, or organization.

Why Target Market?

In your mental health organization or practice, there are a variety of sources of clients, some of greater potential value than others. Like a river, there are sources of clients that flow with tremendous volume and consistency, but there are also rivulets of clients that feed the larger flow. Using the image of managed care as the river, for example, we see the case manager as a rivulet. You have to attend to the rivulets even though they're small, or else the larger river may dry up.

In the very recent past—and even in some areas of the country today—the rivulets of clients were many and varied: friends, churches, schools, advertising, as well as physicians and other clinicians, to name a few. But with the spread of MCOs, we have seen a continuing decline in the variety of referral sources directing clients to therapy. The primary reason for this has been the change in how our healthcare is being delivered, as employers are significantly impacted by the rising cost of healthcare. Along with economics, there is a philosophical issue of which types of healthcare coverage are the obligation of the employer and which should be the responsibility of the employee. Should an employer be financially responsible for providing mental health services to an employee or dependent who wishes to have a deeper understanding of his emotions and how they affect his daily life? Employers have responded to the philosophical shift, altering their benefits packages to provide payment for only those healthcare services that are "medically necessary."

In addition, employers are using "gatekeepers" to ensure that the benefit plan is adhered to. This additional step limits the number of referral sources authorized to approve therapy. Clients can rarely refer themselves if they want their insurance to pay for therapy. "Prior authorization," a term previously reserved for surgery, is now *required* for a patient to see a behavioral healthcare clinician.

This chapter focuses on three of the most influential gatekeepers:

- Managed care companies
- Employers
- Primary care physicians

There are other sources of clients, but in the current and future marketplace the majority of clients will come from these few key sources.

Identifying Your Sources of Referral

Start by gathering information. Begin to identify all the potential referral sources in your service area. This is called generating *lead lists*. Collect the names of contact people representing the gatekeepers in the three main tributaries of client flow: managed care companies, employers, and primary care physicians (Figure 3.1). Time is of the essence, so begin with the most likely sources of potential business.

Check with your chamber of commerce to obtain a list of the largest employers in your area. Even if you believe you know who they are, get the list anyway; companies frequently surprise us with their true size. The chamber list is the source of two main types of leads: managed care companies and employers.

Now it's time for a little phone work. Use your list and call the businesses. We have provided you with an employer survey, or business leads, form (Exhibit 3.1 in the Appendix, intended to be photocopied for your use) to keep track of your calls and information. Your goal is to find out who carries the insurance for these businesses. Start by asking for the secretary in the benefits area or human resources department; they are often a great source of information. The human resources director or whoever handles employee benefits packages can provide you with the desired information quickly. I'm a firm believer that a face-to-face contact is always most productive. But because going face-to-face is time consuming (and frequently the most anxiety-producing for clinicians), phone contact is a good way to gather preliminary information in a time-efficient manner.

You want to find answers to the following questions:

- Which MCOs do you need to contact about being placed on their provider panels?
- Are there any employers who are contracting directly with behavioral health care delivery systems or behavioral health managed care organizations exclusively? This kind of exclusive relationship is known as a *behavioral healthcare carve-out*.
- Which companies are utilizing EAPs in your marketplace, and who are they using?

FIGURE 3.1. CLIENT FLOW.

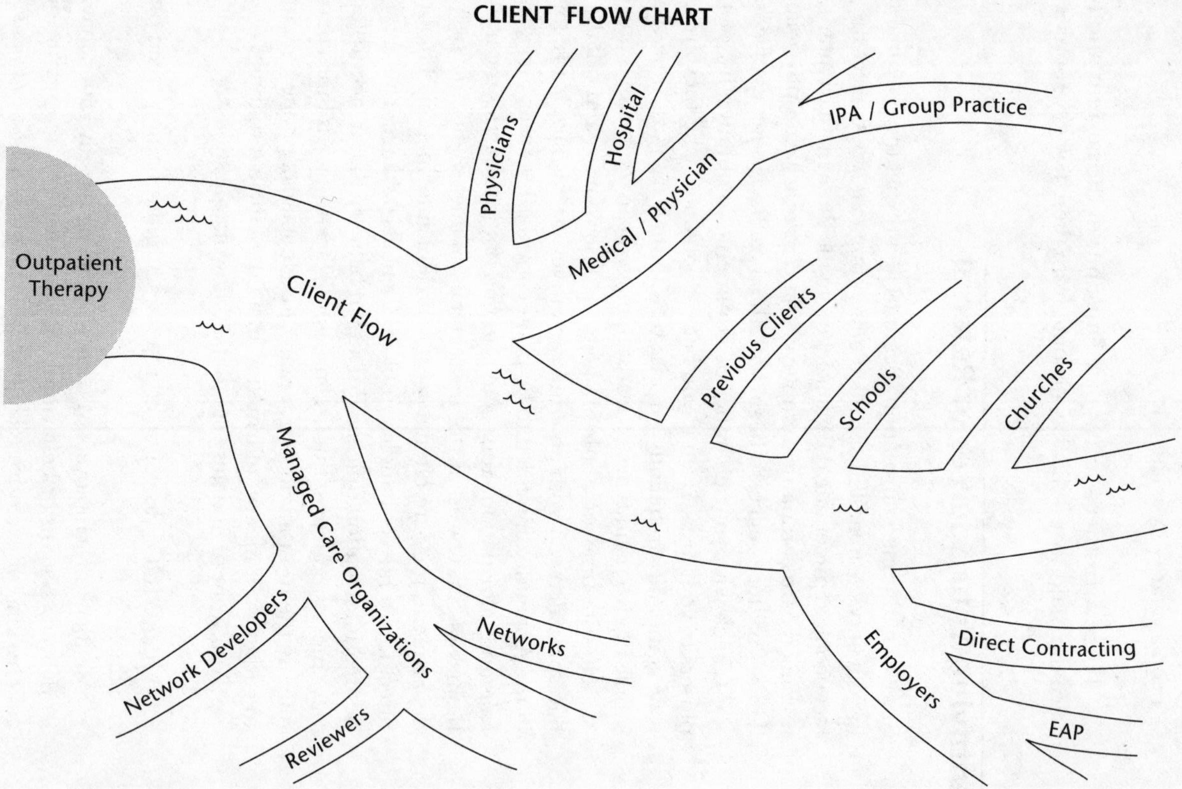

CLIENT FLOW CHART

Outpatient Therapy

Client Flow

Physicians

Hospital

Medical / Physician

IPA / Group Practice

Previous Clients

Schools

Churches

Employers

Direct Contracting

EAP

Managed Care Organizations

Networks

Reviewers

Network Developers

- Which case management or review agencies are providing services in your region?
- Which provider networks are in your service area?
- What opportunities exist with each employer?

This is not the time to tell employers about your services. You're doing a needs assessment to determine what possibilities might exist for you.

You can lead into the questions by saying something like: "My name is Bob Smith. I'm the Director of Network Development for Ohio Regional Mental Health Providers. We are trying to determine if our organization is on the appropriate insurance panels for our community. Because you're a large employer, I'd like to ask you a couple of questions regarding your insurance coverage for mental/nervous disorders [insurance talk for behavioral health coverage]. Do you have a couple of minutes now to answer a few questions?"

Don't be put off if they don't want to take the time to talk. Ask if you can have an appointment, or find out when would be a good time to call back. If they still respond with a no, ask, "Perhaps a secretary or assistant could spend a few minutes with me?" This is your need, not theirs, so be persistent and persuasive, but not pushy. Make them feel that you need and value what they have to say.

Although you are using the local or regional chamber of commerce list to gather MCOs and EAP information, remember that many national organizations (such as Fortune 500 companies) may not join the local Chamber even though they have a large number of local employees. Therefore you need to obtain employer lists from other sources beside the Chamber of Commerce. Often the local city business journal or newspaper publishes lists of the largest public and private employers annually. Another resource is the Judy Diamond Directory, which sells lists of self-insured companies by city.

Typically national employers have their insurance coverage through a large company with a national network, or they may be self-funded. Also, national companies tend to contract for EAP services with a national EAP organization, but they may have a regional EAP located out of the regional office, or a regional office that contracts with local clinicians to provide EAP services. That's why you need to contact each one to find out how they are structured.

If a large employer is self-funded, a direct contracting opportunity exists. *Self-funded* means the company insures itself. Usually these are large organizations with many employees, such as General Dynamics Corporation in Falls Church, Virginia. Note that many school districts are also self-funded. Basically the way self-funding works is employees pay into an insurance fund which is maintained by an administrator, who then pays for healthcare services out of the fund. Exhibit 3.1

in the Appendix includes questions specifically about self-funded companies to assist you in gathering information on this opportunity for direct contracting.

If the employer is unable to provide you with the phone number or address of the MCO or EAP, you will need to find these numbers by going to the library and looking in a directory of HMOs and PPOs (preferred provider organizations). Or look for journals in the managed care and EAP fields. Another source of addresses and phone numbers is the local newspaper or business journal; they frequently publish a list of the largest MCOs in your region. Many of these companies have an 800 number and can be reached through the 800 operator. The Employee Assistance Professional Association (EAPA) in Arlington, Virginia, can provide contact information for EAPs in your area; their phone number is (703) 522–6272.

The third major source of client flow is the primary care physician group. This tributary consists of independent physicians, physician groups, psychiatric groups, and hospitals.

If you have a psychiatric hospital in your service area, become familiar with its admitting staff. Call the hospital and ask for the name of the head of the admitting department. Also, find out if they have a crisis team. These team members come into contact with many potential clients who generally require referral to a therapist. The director of managed care at the psychiatric hospital is a good name to collect during your phone work. This person is frequently asked to recommend clinicians for managed care panels and is surely the most knowledgeable individual concerning behavioral healthcare MCOs operating in your marketplace.

Physicians are a primary source of referrals. Primary care physicians (PCPs) act as the gatekeepers for many HMOs. Physicians may have an individual office, or they may work in a group practice. They may also have a group practice "without walls," operating as a group but having separate offices. The physicians operating in a group or an independent practice association (IPA) may have a name such as Doctors Medical Group and an administrator, depending on the size of the group. Call the local medical/surgical hospital's communications department and ask about local physician groups or IPAs. Medical societies are another great source of physician information; they also publish directories of their physician members. The directory should list the physicians by specialty and give their names, addresses, and phone numbers. This is very helpful because you want to limit your contacts to primary care physicians (PCPs) who specialize in family practice, internal medicine, Ob/Gyn, or pediatrics. As the primary gatekeepers for HMOs, and as HMO utilization grows, PCPs are becoming an increasingly important referral source. Additionally, pharmaceutical companies, as well as managed care organizations, are recognizing and training PCPs to be the primary screeners and triage specialists for major affective disorders, such as depression.

If this type of interviewing is not your strength, or if you don't have the time, it would be wise to hire a marketing professional to conduct these phone interviews for you. To be successful, you need to find a way to gather this information. One way to do this cost-effectively is by sharing the costs of a marketing firm among several clinicians you have relationships with.

Managed Care: The Colorado River of Client Flow

In California's metropolitan areas, MCOs have a 65 percent share of the marketplace. As you research the number of individuals in your market area covered by HMOs and PPOs that limit clients' choice of providers, you can begin to determine how much of your marketing efforts need to be focused on becoming part of these PPO and HMO panels.

MCOs require that you be credentialed and approved for participation in their provider networks if the client plans to bill the insurance provider for therapy. If the insurance company is part of a PPO, the client will be encouraged to see a therapist on the network provider panel, who will provide the therapy for a discounted fee that costs the client less out of pocket. PPOs permit subscribers (employees and their dependents) to choose from therapists on the panel or not; however, usually there is a strong financial incentive to the client to use providers who are part of the PPO.

An HMO will pay for services provided by a panel member only. One hundred percent of the fees for out-of-panel services are paid for by the client. Some clients choose to see a therapist they are familiar with, paying the difference or even the full fee. Generally, employees and their dependents initially resist the restrictions required by the MCO but within a couple of years become familiar with MCO panel members and conform to the requirements.

I caution you not to assume that employees' early resistance to MCOs will result in managed care organizations' failure to grow in your marketplace. MCOs are here to stay. I recommend a proactive approach of collaboration with managed care organizations.

Once you have a list of the MCOs in your area, start making phone calls to all of them. Ask for the person who develops the provider networks for outpatient services. The title varies with each MCO and could be "contract negotiator" or someone in charge of provider development, provider relations, or network development. Your goal is to become a provider. Exhibit 3.2 in the Appendix (meant to be photocopied for your use) should help you collect this information.

The process of getting on panels becomes complicated for many clinicians as they consider the organization's policies, procedures, treatment philosophy, fee schedule, and reputation. I believe you need to get on as many panels as possible. I'm *not* encouraging you to support an unethical company, or one that doesn't value your services or pays you inappropriately. After a merger, today's dog of a company could be tomorrow's star. Procedures also change, and a company's ridiculously low fee of last year may come to look decent in a tough year. We've seen it happen in California. Social workers balking at sixty dollars per session last year are now accepting forty, or twenty-five in Los Angeles! Remember, as a panel member you don't have to accept the patient; you're entitled to say, "I'm sorry, I'm full and can't fit them in until next month. Perhaps another referral would be more expedient." But at least you're on the panel, and the decision of whether or not to accept a patient is *yours*.

For example, an MCO entered our market about six years ago. The company was one of the first behavioral healthcare carve-outs. When they first began managing the care of patients, the clinicians were outraged. The company became very unpopular with the clinical community. Then the MCO was purchased by a larger medical insurance company. The organization's policies of management/case review changed only slightly, but now they had more staff and more accessibility to clinicians. Currently they are considered one of the better payers. Many of the clinicians who refused to become panel members are regretting their decision today, since the panel was closed and has yet to reopen. This story has been repeated, I'm sure, in many markets.

Prior to contacting the network developer at the MCO, determine your niche or specialty as a provider. The next chapter discusses how to go about determining the needs of your community. You will be best served by finding a way to set yourself apart from the other outpatient providers. A word of caution: Don't say you specialize in depression. Everyone works with depression! Your niche may be working with eating disorders, or small children, or substance abuse. You're in luck if you know sign language or speak Hmong. We live in a dynamic society, and the needs of the community are changing. Develop a specialty that will be in demand today *and* tomorrow in your community.

Prepare to discuss your training and experience in brief therapy. If you have any statistics regarding the average length of time a client is in treatment with you, that will be a plus.

The behavioral healthcare industry is also becoming much more outcomes-oriented. This goes beyond patient satisfaction. The purpose of outcomes research is to hold providers accountable for the effectiveness of treatment they render. The most credible outcome studies are those validated using recognized and standardized tools—so don't create your own. Use a measurement tool that is valid, reliable, and recognized by the industry. There are many opportunities to attend seminars and workshops on outcomes studies. The Institute for Behavioral Healthcare is a resource in the San Francisco Bay Area and holds an annual national conference on outcomes measurement. Also check with other professional associations you belong to. Several professional associations—such as the American Mental Health Counselors Association, the American Association of Partial Hospitalization, and the Mental Health Corporation of America—have pilot programs from which you can obtain recommended outcomes tools. In addition, you may also want to ask various MCOs about the tools they are familiar with or are using for small outcomes projects. If you are already measuring your outcomes, you're way ahead of the game, and you should send this information along with your provider application.

If a company says its panel is closed, send your packet anyway. Ask if there are plans to expand the provider panel. Find out if the MCO desires to contract with a group or an IPA. This information is an indicator of where the market is going and whether or not you should consider forming or joining a group. One way to make inroads onto a seemingly closed panel is to find out if they have any regions or locales where they need additional therapists. Occasionally clinicians get on a panel by agreeing to set up satellite offices in underserved areas. You agree to spend one day a week in the area, and they let you onto the panel. This can really work to your advantage and be a profitable venture if you have this kind of flexibility. Lastly, remember that contracts are won and lost annually or biannually. A company may land a major account and need to grow dramatically, thereby creating an immediate demand for more providers. Or they may lose a contract and leave the market. Stay in touch with the company. Send in your application packet and call back every three or four months, to see if there have been any changes.

The Reviewer Rivulet

You made it! You're on! Is the marketing part over yet . . . ? No, not at all. The panel is full of providers; you are just one of many. But don't get discouraged. Look how far you've come. This is character-developing, like what you tell your clients: Change is slow and persistence pays off. Don't look at how far you have to go; just take one step at a time. You are a skilled clinician who is truly an asset to this managed care organization.

An IPA was formed in our community, consisting of psychiatrists and psychologists. Masters-level clinicians were not asked to buy shares or to be contract providers. The IPA began by becoming the exclusive providers for a large, local HMO that supported having only Ph.D.s and M.D.s serving their membership. But as the IPA began marketing itself to other MCOs, the providers found that the lack of masters-level clinicians was a disadvantage. A decision was made to open up the panel to a "select few," basically to promote the fact that they were multidisciplinary. This helped them in garnering more business, but the clients were still being directed to the shareholders. The "select few" felt used and were angry. Some chose to leave the panel, but others stayed on with an eye toward the future and the direction of the marketplace.

The IPA landed another contract, but this employer wanted *reports*! (Note the power of the employer!) The reports needed to show how many subscribers were being seen by M.D.s, Ph.D.s, and masters-level clinicians. The payer/employer was paying fee-for-service and knew that masters-level clinicians were less costly. Consequently, the employer directed the IPA to use M.D.s only for medication management, psychologists only for testing, and masters-level clinicians for therapy. Guess what. . . . They needed more masters-level clinicians, and the panel opened up for this particular contract. This whole process took about three years. Change is slow, but those who persevered benefited in the long run.

In working with case reviewers, you need to stand out in the crowd. That's hard to do when they can't see you and don't know you. You need to sell your skills and expertise to these important referral sources. Let them get to know you, and you them. Try to develop a collaborative relationship with the reviewer/case manager. Personally, I make two "road trips" a year. A road trip is a face-to-face visit with MCO representatives who make referrals and handle case review. I call in advance and arrange to spend about an hour with the provider relations director, or his or her counterpart. Also, meeting the review staff is always beneficial, because this allows them to connect a face with a name. In doing so, you become actual people to each other. The inevitable differences down the road are more easily worked out if the two of you have met and established a relationship. Only once have I encountered an organization that was too busy to spend some time with me.

Either before the meeting or once on-site, you need to find out how the company is organized with regard to the review process. Do they have many reviewers? Are they divided into regions? Will there be an opportunity for you to develop a relationship with the reviewer? Take time to ask the reviewer how they *evaluate* their providers. (Evaluate??? And you thought grading was over when you got out of school. . . .) Managed care companies have various ways of rating their providers. Some work on a level system; others have an actual grading scale.

During a recent consultation with a behavioral health MCO company in the San Francisco Bay Area, I asked if and how they evaluate their providers. The director of provider relations showed me a computer screen with general information such as name, address, specialty, and a *grade*. In the case on screen, the grade was "B+." The director explained, "This provider is doing well. They have a B+." Another screen with a different provider showed an A; the director said, "This guy used to work here." Another screen . . . a C. The provider relations staff told us that every interaction was graded on a scale of 0 to 4 by the person conducting the review. They said they evaluate the providers based upon the organization of the information they are presenting, diagnostic skill, treatment plan, and so on.

Organizations may differ with regard to what they look for and evaluate. One MCO told us they evaluate how quickly a person is seen following a referral. A twenty-four-hour response time is usually worth points. This illustrates why it's critical to know what is important to each company you are providing services for. A clinician with a low score or grade will be more closely scrutinized by the MCO and will be likely to receive fewer referrals.

I'm familiar with another MCO that uses a level system. The MCO requires a clinician to see a predetermined number of clients in order to work their way up the level system. If the clinician is performing up to expectation, there is an increase in autonomy and level. At the highest level, they do not have to be reviewed. The maximum number of sessions is authorized at the beginning. In this case, if you are performing within their expectations consistently, the organization may grant you more latitude in your treatment plan.

You must prove yourself worthy of autonomy by playing the game by their rules. Understanding what they want or expect is the key. Ask them about their philosophy of treatment. Nearly every company wants brief therapy or problem-focused therapy. "Insight"-oriented therapy is a thing of the past if managed care is paying the bill. Remember, the insurance company's goal of treatment is usually to return the clients to their previous level of functioning. For the insurance company, job performance is the issue, not the client's state of mind. A hint for retaining satisfaction in your practice: reserve some treatment time in your schedule to work with clients who will pay cash and want to do insight work. This helps satisfy your need to do some in-depth psychotherapeutic treatment.

Network Rivulet

Some MCOs contract with an established network of providers, instead of developing their own. Developing a network is a long and arduous task. Network developers must establish a system of locating outpatient providers. The Yellow Pages are sometimes used, but judging therapists' reputations and practice standards from this source is an unknown. Frequently the network developers call the local psychiatric hospital and ask the director of managed care to make recommendations of prospective panel providers or they inquire about the practice of a particular clinician. Once a network developer has determined the names of potential providers, each must be contacted and sent an application. The application process involves credentialing providers based upon the network's criteria of participation. As you can see, this process is very time consuming.

Many states require an MCO to have a provider panel in place in order to sell their product in a marketplace. Companies have emerged that are just networks. These companies sell their network panels to the MCO. A network may also have products of their own that they sell, such as case management services, and so forth. And some MCOs sell their network. Thus you could be a provider for a particular MCO and find out you are now a provider for another company because your services have been sold to a new payer.

Employer Tributary: Channeling the Flow of Clients

As mentioned earlier, employers are the drivers of the changes we are experiencing in the healthcare market. Employers are the customers of MCOs. Managed care has certainly contained the costs to the employer, but in many cases it has not saved employers as much money as they initially thought it would. This is because the MCOs have hired entire staffs of clinicians to provide case management services. Direct contracting between clinicians and employers cuts out the insurance company or MCO middleman and limits their control, because the case management services are provided by the contracted clinician group. An entire chapter could be devoted to the how-to's of this process, so here I give you just the highlights.

Direct-Contracting Rivulet

Direct contracting with an employer is a viable option in two circumstances. The first is in markets where employers are seeking to hold down mental health benefit costs but are not ready for a completely limited choice in mental health benefits as with an HMO. In this circumstance, employers are open to contracting directly with a PPO made up of a large selection of strategically located practitioners and psychiatric hospitals. These employers wish to preserve consumer choice while holding down costs.

Alternatively, in more-progressive managed care markets, where MCOs have a firm foothold and the community has become familiar with the MCO process, employers are exploring further cost-saving opportunities through direct contracting with providers and cutting out the costs of the middleman.

In both cases, direct contracting involves a group or large number of outpatient clinicians teaming up with one or more psychiatric hospitals to provide a full continuum of behavioral healthcare. This could include providing EAP services, but at a minimum the direct contract would cover outpatient through inpatient services. The team contracting directly with an employer needs to be prepared to address several issues:

Abundant choice of providers

Wide geographic coverage, with outpatient offices conveniently located no further than fifteen to twenty minutes from employer locations and employee homes

Alternative pricing options

Twenty-four-hour access systems

Case management

Quality assurance

Credentialing of providers

Grievance procedures

Outcomes measures

In other words, the provider group becomes the managed care firm. This takes significant systems development and financial investment on the part of the providers. This option is only recommended if you are part of a large, integrated delivery system.

Employee Assistance Rivulet

In lieu of a generous behavioral healthcare benefit, some employers have chosen to enhance the Employee Assistance Program, using this program as some or all of the outpatient behavioral healthcare benefits package.

Pull out your list of EAPs and EAP personnel, the one you developed as you were calling the employers. EAPs are a great group to target because they are clinicians who frequently need to refer clients out and can't or usually don't refer to themselves. Many employers contract with EAPs as a means of controlling their behavioral healthcare costs. The EAP's goal is to intervene with employees who are experiencing problems which are affecting their job performance. The issues could be anything from substance abuse problems to marital or financial difficulties. The primary issue is that their job performance is being impacted. Employees can refer themselves or be referred by a supervisor. The EAP's level of involvement varies with the employer's expectations and the definition of the role of their EAP. When you are surveying your employer contacts and asking questions about the insurance plan (Exhibit 3.1 in the Appendix), ask if they use an EAP. If the answer is yes, proceed with gathering additional information on the Business Leads Form.

In asking whether the EAP's function includes providing wellness seminars, make a note to yourself: an opportunity may exist for you to develop a relationship with the EAP by offering to perform this service. Some EAPs provide their own wellness seminars, but others may have the flexibility to coordinate speakers on topics outside of their areas of expertise. You don't want to compete with them; you want to develop a relationship with the EAP so they will learn more about you and refer employees to you for treatment. One way to do this would be to offer to provide a wellness seminar *through* the EAP. In doing so, you help the EAP personnel look good to the employer, and they in turn have the opportunity to see you demonstrate your skill at presenting. If they don't attend your presentation, end the session with a satisfaction survey, the results of which you can forward to the EAP. (Of course, the survey responses will all be positive, and the EAP will want more!) At the bottom of the satisfaction survey for the employees in attendance, include a list of other topics you could offer. Ask the employees to circle topics of interest. If the survey results are uniformly good, mail the actual surveys to the EAP person. This is always more impressive than a summary you prepare. Be sure to draw the EAP's attention to the employees' requests and to your willingness to present on these additional topics.

If the EAP is local and provides its own wellness seminars, meet with the personnel anyway. Remember, you are a skilled professional, and this EAP will be thankful to be made aware of your services. You should have the information you collected from your employer survey; use it to lead you through your own needs assessment before making the appointment. You may be asking yourself, What do the EAP clinicians need to make their job easier? Ask them, "What is your role as an EAP director?" They may answer, "We assess and refer. . . ." Or "We assess and provide up to three sessions of counseling." The employee assistance personnel providing the services may answer your questions differently than the employer you spoke with. Confirm the information you received from the employer; exercise the skills you have as a trained listener. Ask open-ended questions until you uncover a need you can fill. How can you fit in? Tell them!

Primary Care Physicians

Managed care organizations (such as HMOs) that are not behavioral healthcare carve-outs frequently delegate to physicians the task of authorizing a referral to a therapist. In this situation, physicians act as the control system, which allows a patient to make an appointment with a mental health professional. Thus the gatekeepers are primary care physicians who may or may not be knowledgeable regarding mental health issues, signs, or symptoms. It is essential that a good working relationship be developed with these physicians.

As clinicians, we feel managed care has seriously impacted our financial well-being, as well as our ability to provide the type of therapy we were trained to provide. We have joined the ranks of many physicians who have seen an overall decline of 30 percent in their income. The fact of our shared condition presents some opportunities for clinicians to work with physicians for mutual benefit.

Physicians are forming group practices, Independent Practice Associations (IPAs), Physician Hospital Organizations (PHOs), and so on, so they will be in a position to capitate with an MCO or employer. For those of you still enjoying a marketplace whose MCO penetration is only 5–10 percent or so, let me translate. Physicians are joining together in formal groups so they can negotiate agreements with an insurance company/employer. These agreements stipulate an agreed-upon amount of money the physicians will receive each month to treat all the subscribers (employees, dependents, and retirees) covered under that insurance plan in the service area. The treatment providers, therefore, become "cost centers" instead of "revenue centers." Every time they provide treatment, the cost comes out of the pot of money they received that month from the insurance company to provide care. If they don't need to provide a service or treatment, the money is "unspent" and becomes profit for the physicians.

How do therapists fit into this equation? Well, if you can provide a psychological service that keeps a patient from needing more medical services, you have benefited the physician financially, and the patient personally. The term is "medical cost offset." You are offsetting the cost of providing additional medical treatment by focusing on the possible underlying cause of the problem, such as depression. A perfect example is the patient having a panic attack who shows up in a hospital emergency room. The hospital conducts medical tests to determine if there is an organic cause for the symptoms. If the cause is panic or anxiety, they are unable to find anything wrong and send the patient home. If the medical facility is capitated for such costs, it is to their advantage to look for the root cause of the visit and treat that cause. Marketing your services to emergency room physicians or the social services staff of a hospital is therefore a natural link. In practice, most patients are currently referred back to their primary physician without mention of treating the anxiety.

Physician Rivulet

Developing a relationship with a physician takes time. Most are busy and are reluctant to meet with you—because the benefits (for them) are not clear. Start with the office manager or nurse. These are individuals with invaluable information, who frequently have tremendous influence over the practice. They should not be overlooked. The nurse can tell you how the practice operates with regard to referrals for services not provided by the physician. I have included a Physician Referral Form you can use to keep track of physicians you have contacted (Exhibit 3.3 in the Appendix; to be photocopied for your use). Sometimes the physician doesn't make referrals, and the task is delegated to a nurse or other office personnel. The doctor will say something like, "This patient needs to see a dermatologist," and the nurse makes the decision as to which dermatologist. Thus, in the case of behavioral healthcare, the nurse or office manager might tell the doctor about a great experience she or he or a friend had with a particular therapist, and thereby influence where the doctor refers. Make sure you learn how a physician's office operates, and don't underestimate the power of the nurse or office manager.

Developing a relationship with a physician can also start when you share a patient who is in therapy with you. *Always* get a release to speak with the client's primary care physician first. Contact the physician to introduce yourself and let him know you are treating one of his patients for a psychological disorder. Follow up with a summary note to the physician stating your findings and recommendations. Doctors are trained to look for pathology. They frequently miss psychiatric problems because they traditionally don't test for them.

As the marketing director for a psychiatric hospital and a clinician, I knew that physicians were seeing patients in their practice every day who had undiagnosed psychological problems. But when I would meet with a doctor to tell him about our services, I would frequently hear, "I rarely see patients in my practice who would need hospitalization for psychiatric problems."

Consequently, I started getting releases from every patient who was admitted to our facility to provide their primary care physicians with a copy of the history and physical completed during their hospitalization, along with the discharge summary. My goal was to educate them and heighten their awareness of just how many patients they see daily who have a psychiatric diagnosis. I would hand deliver the released information, creating an opportunity to remind them of our services. When I began this process, our facility was receiving about 4 percent of our referrals from physicians. Within two years, the percentage jumped to 17 percent. The key was education and visibility.

Now our task has shifted to educating physicians about early intervention in the treatment of common mental disorders, as a means of saving money for the physician and the MCO. We've had some success recently with primary care physicians when we encouraged them to use the ZUNG depression inventory for patients mentioning symptoms of depression. Those who are in tune with psychiatric disorders or have a holistic approach to medicine have found it a valuable tool which opens up further areas of discussion.

Physicians are feeling the time crunch of getting the patient in and out of the office quickly. Doctors used to be able to spend time with patients, learning about their families and the individual conditions which might contribute to medical issues. In order to regain the income they used to earn, physicians are dealing with the need to see more patients in a day since they are being paid less per patient. If a physician can refer a patient to you, you have saved him or her time and money.

Developing a relationship with a physician takes time. Send journal information you find on medical cost offset, or the cost of treating undiagnosed depression. A new hot topic is depression in the elderly. Literature reports that 26 percent of the senior population suffers from undiagnosed depression. You can also research which physicians in your community specialize in geriatric patients and start to educate them. Refer to your professional journals for appropriate articles, or go to the library and photocopy articles on depression or anxiety that relate to geriatric health. Start sending the information to physicians periodically. You will see a return from this effort.

Physician Group/IPA Rivulet

Another possibility that may exist within some markets is to join a medical group practice as the staff therapist. This could involve leasing space and using their central support services for billing and appointments and so on. This would take some salesmanship to convince a group practice administrator that a staff therapist would be an advantage. But having someone available for consultation or evaluation and to provide wellness seminars could be sold as value-added services to patients and physicians.

Some managed care companies that own group practices have hired clinicians for their clinics, thus keeping everything in-house. Here the clinician is an employee of the HMO, just like the physicians. It's referred to in California as the "Kaiser model," after its use at Kaiser Permanente. Referrals are generated by the HMO. Patients needing mental health services are required to come to the organization's providers. You are an employee of the HMO earning a salary with benefits, and the HMO sets your hours as in any employer/employee relationship. Some HMOs are hiring part-time clinicians. This provides the security of a salary, but you still have the opportunity to maintain a private practice if you so desire. The HMO might have a particular method of treating patients with certain disorders, which would limit your autonomy in how you choose to work with a patient. Others may not have such standards and require only that you be subject to review if a case seems excessively long.

Hospital Rivulet

The criteria for admission to a psychiatric hospital have become more acute. Patients frequently must demonstrate a failure to respond to outpatient treatment in order to be admitted to a more intensive program. The admitting staff at psychiatric hospitals need to refer more and more patients to outpatient therapists. Providing hospital staff with a current list of your managed care contracts, and making them aware of your specialties, will help you generate clients from this referral source. Be visible. Apply for privileges and become a member of the hospital staff.

A psychiatric hospital that has a community crisis-response team is also a source of potential referrals. Clinicians operating in this capacity respond to calls from emergency rooms, schools, doctors' offices, retirement centers, or any organization that has a person they feel is in crisis and needs to be evaluated by a clinician. Crisis team members can be a part of the regular hospital staff, or they can be moonlighting clinicians. (Of course, if they were clinicians in private practice, referral to their own practices would be questionable.) However, participation as a crisis team member provides the clinician with visibility within the psychiatric hospital, with the admissions office, and in the organizations requesting crisis services. Developing a relationship with these team members, and making them aware of your services or areas of expertise, can generate referrals to your practice as well.

As mentioned earlier, the director of managed care, or whoever is contracting for MCO services for a psychiatric hospital, is frequently asked by MCOs entering the market for the names of clinicians who are "managed-care friendly." Directors recommend clinicians they are familiar with and who they feel would make a good partner with the MCO. Remember, the director is also trying to develop a relationship with the MCO. His or her concern is to recommend clinicians who will refer to his or her hospital if inpatient care is indicated. Let the director know about your practice patterns and that you are open to referring to his or her hospital when appropriate. A director will not recommend clinicians who are aligned with a competing facility. This becomes a dilemma if you refer to more than one facility.

◆ ◆ ◆

This chapter began by describing a clinician starting out in a private practice who chose her office location without regard to potential referrals from her neighbors. Clinicians locating their offices in a medical area have a built-in opportunity to develop a relationship with the physicians/hospitals and their staff. There isn't a better place to locate your office than alongside or within close proximity to medical professionals.

Now take a deep breath. Don't get overwhelmed with everything you have to know and do. Start with the areas of greatest potential first. If your service already has heavy penetration by managed care in your area, I would recommend that you begin with the MCO having the largest local membership. A relationship with an employer or medical professional will not benefit you unless you are able to treat the patients being referred. If you are not in a major MCO market, physicians can become a primary referral source; keeping abreast of which MCOs are busy contacting physicians can give you inside information on MCOs planning to enter the market. Then you contact the MCOs regarding behavioral healthcare.

If your strategy is to capture clients who will pay cash, be prepared to discount your fees to be equal to what the client would have to pay if billing the insurance company. Realize also that when MCOs enter the market, and even after they have developed and maintained their presence, the "cash clients" become the strategic focus of the majority of clinicians. This is largely due to denial of the effect of MCOs on clinicians' practices. Ninety percent of clinicians start out with this strategy. In most metropolitan areas, MCOs will soon become the primary payers of healthcare services. This strategy of exclusively targeting the cash clients will work for only a small minority of clinicians. Read the literature, be proactive, and keep an eye on the future of healthcare in America. A continuous stream of clients is available to those who persevere and find creative ways to open the locks and dams and direct the flow of business.

Notes

P. 31, *Judy Diamond Directory:* You can inquire about this directory by calling (800) 231–0669.

P. 32, *directory of HMOs and PPOs:* There is a national HMO/PPO directory from Medical Device Register that you can purchase by calling (800) 222–3045.

CHAPTER FOUR

DECIDING WHAT SERVICES TO PROVIDE

Product Planning and Market Research

Jeri Davis

I n product planning, it is important to keep one step ahead of the market to en-sure that your products and services remain viable. Many profound changes are happening in both healthcare and behavioral healthcare that are revolutionizing both what psychiatric care will look like and how it will be delivered. The major forces of managed care that are driving most of the changes in behavioral healthcare today are (1) continuing pressure nationwide to control and lower mental healthcare costs and (2) the advancement of computer technology, which is allowing us to track and evaluate treatment interventions faster and in more depth than ever before.

These factors have far-reaching impact on what you will be doing in the near future.

What Will Behavioral Healthcare Treatment Look Like in the Year 2000?

Given this rapid period of change, it's difficult to predict exactly how behavioral healthcare will look four years from now. However, the managed care trends listed in the following chart are well under way and can be expected to continue. Use the chart to get ideas on how to turn managed care trends into new business opportunities.

Note: Jill Buckingham, M.B.A., provided the Sample Demographic Analysis on pp. 49–51.

Key National Managed Care Trends

Opportunities for Behavioral Healthcare Practitioners

1. Increasing use of outpatient brief-therapy models, group interventions, and non-facility-based treatment methods.

1. Develop and promote your skills in these areas.

2. Tremendous push toward using lower cost therapeutic interventions, and greater demand for outcome studies to verify the success of these interventions.

2. Verify and promote the effectiveness of your services by participating in outcomes studies. The best way to do this is to link up with other providers to share costs and compare results.

3. More and earlier detection and treatment of psychiatric disorders will take place in the primary care physician's office.

   - This means that less of this type of work will be done by psychiatrists.
   - Primary care physicians are trained to do medications management but do not typically have the time or expertise to do psychiatric counseling.

3. Investigate ways to work more closely with primary care physicians, and develop referral relationships with them.

   Examples:
   - Share office space.
   - Subcontract to provide individual or group counseling in physicians' offices.
   - Provide crisis evaluations.
   - Join multispecialty practices as partners or contract employees.

4. Growing orientation toward treating the mind and body together.

4. Develop services that demonstrably impact recovery of individuals with chronic or acute medical problems.

5. Increasing growth of regional and statewide integrated delivery systems which include managed behavioral healthcare organizations.

5. Look at ways to deliver services within local healthcare systems. This may be accomplished through practice affiliations, for example, joining a health system's IPA or PPO, or becoming an employee.

6. Dramatic rise in managed care organizations' involvement in large public-sector contracts:

6. Promote your effectiveness and experience working with these populations.

Medicaid, Medicare, and the implementation of managed care
principles in the public sector.

7. National managed care organizations in behavioral healthcare are
going through major growth
phases, adding new divisions and
lines of business.

7. Determine how you can best fit
into these expansion plans and
what new services you can help
them provide.

8. Growth in geriatric services.

8. Develop specialty skills and experience in this area.

9. Expanding focus on wellness and
early intervention. (These efforts
may not be part of traditional
benefit packages. Rather, these
may be value-added services
provided by employers, EAPs,
and/or insurance companies at
the worksite.

9. Investigate ways to deliver these
services via contracts with employers, EAPs, and/or insurance
companies.

Deciding which of the above opportunities to pursue first requires researching your local market and prospective customers. Different markets move much
faster than others in incorporating new trends. For example, such states as Florida,
California, Texas, and Minnesota are leading the country in healthcare reform.
Areas that are primarily rural, on the other hand, may never incorporate some
managed care trends, or they may develop unique solutions to managed care
because of the scarcity of services.

Similarly, individual customers, such as decision makers within behavioral
healthcare MCOs or physician practices, are open to new ideas mainly when they
feel a need to change. Therefore you must keep abreast of what is happening in
your market area and among your targeted customer groups so that you can develop and sell services when the market is ready to buy them. The following information helps you accomplish this.

Five Steps for Product Planning

Step 1: Profile the consumers in your service area and identify the services they might need.

Contact your local chamber of commerce to obtain a profile of the people who
live in your city. Typically, they provide free of charge a newcomer's welcome package that gives you demographic and employment data on the local area. From this

demographic information, you can learn the characteristics of the population in terms of age, race, income, and employment categories.

Demographic Information

Use demographic information to answer the following questions:

- Which segments of the marketplace—Hispanic, elderly, aging baby boomer— are growing or underserved?
- Is there enough of a population base in my immediate service area to meet my business objectives? Do I need to expand my services to a secondary geographic area because of too much competition or too few consumers for the specialties I serve?
- What services should I be thinking about offering in the future, given the changing demographics of my service area?

Sample Demographic Analysis

Here is a fictitious example of a demographic analysis, for Centertown, a Midwestern city.

The service area is defined as a thirty-mile radius around the provider's location. This encompasses the entire metropolitan area, including Hampton County, parts of Boone, Wayne, and Clareville Counties in Ohio; and part of Clareborn County, Indiana.

If one looks a little wider, within a ninety-mile radius are several large population centers including metropolitan Columbia (Ohio), Indianaport (Indiana), and Louistown (Kentucky). Consider marketing to regional managed care companies that may have large contracts in these major cities and need providers throughout the region.

Population Trends. Although there was an overall population growth in the Centertown service area of 3.3 percent from 1,401,135 in 1980 to 1,447,131 in 1990, population is projected to decline 0.13 percent between 1995 and 2000.

Total number of households increased 3 percent between 1990 and 1995. This paradox (less population, but more households) is due to lifestyle changes, with more "single" individuals making up a household. This is principally persons at two points along the age spectrum: young singles or divorced adults without children, and older, widowed persons.

Average family size is projected to decrease also, from 3.34 in 1990 to 3.10 in 2000.

In terms of age distinction, the groups with the highest growth rates 1990–2000 in Centertown are

Age 30–44   24 percent annual growth rate

Age 65+   13 percent annual growth rate

In terms of minority populations, Centertown saw virtually no change in the years 1980–1995. Blacks remain the only significant minority, at 12 percent of the population. This compares to the national average of 11 percent. What differs from nationwide norms in Centertown is the absence of any other minorities in meaningful numbers.

Family households mirror U.S. norms:

Married couples   60 percent

Single female head   11 percent

Single male head   2 percent

Income. The annual rate of income growth in this area is almost 50 percent less than the U.S. annual rate. Per capita income is 6 percent higher in Centertown than the average elsewhere in the country. Although families on average earn more here, there is very little upward movement in income levels. Average household income for 1990 was $34,123 in Centertown, versus $32,686 nationwide. In terms of income distribution in Centertown, there is a swell at the $35,000–50,000 range (21 percent), but most households make less than $35,000 (57 percent).

Sources of income are primarily from wages and salaries (79 percent of households declare this source). Eight percent of households have some public assistance income, and 26 percent have social security income (same as the U.S. norms).

Employment. The Centertown area breakdown by occupation is

Executive and professional	23 percent
Technical and sales	14 percent
Clerical	18 percent
Service	25 percent
Farming	1 percent
Operators	14 percent
Laborers	5 percent
	100 percent

Synopsis and Implications. Here is a synopsis of this demographic analysis and its implications for new-product development in behavioral healthcare service provision.

- Population growth has reached a plateau. This means that you will increase your market share only at the expense of other providers. Creative programming and excellent customer service are needed to garner market share from other providers.
- The population is shifting toward more young to middle-aged adults (30–44) and elderly (65+). This indicates a need either for programs for people in their prime child-rearing years or for geriatric programs. Keep in mind though, that only 60 percent of family households are married couples.
- Many nontraditional types of households exist: adult same-sex households, unmarried couples, related adults living together, intergenerational families, etc. These nontraditional households point the way toward innovative programming, such as help for the "sandwich" generation—those caring for children and aging parents in the same household.
- Income is not growing and unemployment is. Most households (averaging three people) earn less than $35,000 annually collectively. This means that to attract new clients, fees must be reasonable.

This area should be investigated for possible expanded office and service locations.

Local Trends in Managed Care

Additional demographic information important to you is what percentage of the population in your service area is covered by an HMO or behavioral healthcare managed care organization (BHMCO), and how this percentage has grown or changed over the last few years. This will tell you how much of your market you need to target through MCOs, and what percentage you can target for self-pay or full-choice referrals. The best source for this information is from the HMOs and BHMCOs having a large share of business in your area. They are likely to assiduously monitor both their own and their competitors' total number of lives covered.

The way to obtain this information is simply to ask the network manager or a sales representative, "How many lives do you cover in the area under your HMO/BHMCO plan? How does this compare to the number of lives covered by your competitors? How have these percentages changed over the last few years?" These are questions that you can easily incorporate into an interview and that ideally are asked in person.

Managed care organizations will share this information with you willingly if they perceive that you are a potential panel member, customer, or referral source. I routinely collect this information around the country for various clients. When speaking with a network manager, I usually say, "I'm doing a market analysis for a client and would like to know more about your organization." This strategy works well, especially if my client is an organization that the MCO would like to work with.

The key to success in information gathering is to use a positive, confident, and inquisitive tone of voice that communicates to the interviewee that you have important issues to discuss. I try to make the individual feel it is worth his or her time and effort to give me the information I'm seeking. I'm not pushy, since this would be a turn-off. Rather, I'm genuinely interested in what the person has to say. I cannot emphasize enough here how important a pleasant manner and approach are. In the last five years I have averaged over 90 percent success in obtaining information from top-level executives using this technique.

Another source for this information is the local business journal or newspaper. Annually, these publications print a list of HMOs, the number of lives they cover, and their major accounts, along with other useful information. The two problems with these lists are that they go out-of-date very quickly, and some companies tend to overreport data to look better publicly. So if you use this source, be sure to verify the information.

Lifestyle Profile

Now think about the types of people in the geographic area you want to service. What are their lifestyles? What needs or stresses are created by their lifestyle choices or the pressures of today's economy and workforce? These needs are referred to as psychodemographics; they greatly influence what services people buy.

There are actually national data bases that profile consumers according to psychodemographic categories and purchasing behavior, such as "young marrieds without children—dual income" and "young married—single income." These data bases are very expensive to access. So unless you are working with a large marketing budget, just use local newspaper and journal articles to identify some lifestyle segments you may want to develop targeted services for.

Following are two examples of lifestyle categories of individuals who are very similar demographically but who differ dramatically in their service needs and purchases based on psychodemographics.

1. Young single households (20–30, single income over $35,000 annually)

Healthcare needs:

Preemployment physicals

Episodic, emergency care

Ob/Gyn checkups

Help in selecting a primary care physician

Sports medicine

Group selects primary physician according to:

Good recommendation

Like M.D. once they meet him or her

Convenience—parking, after work hours, no waiting time

Group's lifestyle:

Spend money on fun and entertainment

Provider can communicate with group through:

Work: employee newsletters, on-site workshops, employee lunchroom flyers

Radio and local print media

Direct mail

National online data bases

Lifestyle and psychological product lines this group may need:

Workshops, support groups, and individual counseling on stress, depression, anxiety, phobias, or addictions

Workshops, support groups, and individual counseling on a variety of relationship issues

Workshops, support groups, and individual counseling on weight control and smoking cessation

Career counseling, testing, placement, and workshops on building self-esteem

Dealing with separation issues: leaving home, relocation, major loss due to death or accident

Workshops, support groups, and individual counseling on such issues as "Becoming an Adult in the '90s: Stresses and Responsibilities"

As you can see in the above examples, I have suggested a series of services you could offer, all dealing with specific subject matter. This is called a *product line*. The goal of a product line is to offer a range of programs to meet whatever depth or type of service a customer might need in a particular problem/product category.

2. Young marrieds with small children (20–30; dual income over $40,000 annually)

Healthcare needs:

   Routine checkups

   Minor illness treatment—colds, childhood illnesses

   Emergency care—broken bones

   Help in selecting a pediatrician

Group selects primary physician according to:

   Good recommendation

   Like M.D. once they meet him or her

   Convenience: twenty-four-hour physician response, short waiting time, front office staff helpful and friendly

   Weekend hours very important for pediatric services

Lifestyle:

   Spend money on children: clothes, school, toys, healthcare, and child care

Provider can communicate with audience through:

   Work: employer newsletters, on-site workshops, lunchroom flyers

   Radio and local print media

   Local parent's publications

   Direct mail

   National online data bases

   Schools

   Pediatricians

Lifestyle and psychological product lines this group may need:

   Workshops, support groups, and individual counseling on parenting and marital issues

   Career counseling, testing, placement, and workshops on building self-esteem

   Workshops, support groups, and individual counseling dealing with stresses of major life choices: leaving workforce temporarily to be a full-time parent, juggling demanding job and home life, coping when one spouse loses a job

Workshops, support groups, and individual counseling on stress, depression, anxiety, phobias, or addictions

In deciding which products to offer, another very important lifestyle factor to consider is whether or not people have time to utilize your services. A busy mom or dad, working long hours and handling child care duties, is not going to have many free evenings or weekends to attend workshops. You need to give careful consideration to the timing and location of your services, so that consumers who would like to utilize them do not have to overcome too many obstacles to do so. The severe time constraints on many Americans creates a demand for self-help services people can use at home, such as videos, online programs, and in-home care.

Now it's your turn to think of some creative new services for target consumer groups in your area. This is a fun activity to do with friends, spouses, and colleagues. Let your imagination go! Don't rule out any ideas until you have had a chance to explore whether the market is ripe to proceed further.

Step 2: Verify that consumers will buy your new services.

OK, you have come up with some great new service ideas. Before you run out and try to sell them, there are some intermediary steps which need to be completed.

First, you need to check to see if prospective customer groups really want the services you believe they want. You verify demand through qualitative and quantitative marketing research. These techniques are described later in this chapter.

Second, you need to find out what services (if any) prospective buyers are now using to fulfill the need you have identified. Most new products are improvements or replacements for those products or services people were using previously. You need to identify how your new idea is a demonstrable improvement over what people are currently using, so they will buy your product instead. Here are some common service improvements that cause people to switch:

- More convenient location
- Lower price
- Better service
- Faster service
- More effective results
- Easier to obtain
- Easier to use
- Requires lower initial financial commitment
- Better packaging (for example, a workshop that has a more appealing title)

Think of the times when you switched services. What motivated you to change? Use your own experience to help identify service improvement opportunities. The two formal ways to identify service improvement opportunities are through the qualitative and quantitative marketing research process, and through carefully studying your competition.

Qualitative and Quantitative Marketing Research

Qualitative marketing research encompasses gathering information regarding people's feelings and perceptions about the services they buy. It is used most effectively to understand

- Specific characteristics of a program that will make it more desirable than current offerings
- Satisfaction and dissatisfaction with your service, as well as with competitive programs
- Perceptions and attitudes about new program ideas in terms of features, pricing, delivery systems, and promotional techniques

Qualitative research usually takes the form of one-to-one interviews, small group interviews of only two to three people (in addition to the moderator), or focus groups. Focus groups are in-depth roundtable discussions of product issues. They are usually composed of eight to twelve people, plus a discussion leader.

The size of the group depends on several factors: the amount of information you want from each individual, the confidentiality of the information you want to share and/or obtain, and the compatibility and availability of target customers/decision makers. A one-to-one interview gives you the most information, typically one or two hours' worth per person. The focus group gives you the least information: five to ten minutes of information per person over a two-hour period.

For example, in developing a psychiatric product for primary care physicians in your area, one-to-one interviews would be preferable to a group format. Since confidentiality is very important, the information-gathering process is best accomplished one-to-one. Also, you will get much more information about an individual physician's practice if you are speaking to that person alone. Lastly, it is very difficult to get a group of physicians to find a common time to meet. Hence, for confidentiality and logistics, individual interviews make the most sense with primary care physicians.

Whatever forum you use, you should gather information from a minimum of fifteen to twenty people. When designing a qualitative survey, think of the who, what, when, and where of the purchasing process. Include such questions as

- Who are the decision makers for this service?
- What are the features that will make the service most attractive to you the customer?
- What is a fair price to charge?
- When is the best time to offer this service?
- Where is the best place to locate this service?
- What are the best ways to let you know about this service?

The specific questions you ask may vary. What is important, however, is to thoroughly uncover what people will buy and which features are critical for a successful sale.

Because you have gathered qualitative information from only a small group of individuals, you cannot generalize the findings to all similar customers. This is the purpose of *quantitative research,* to verify demand for the service needs and features you've uncovered. In this step you want to count how many prospective customers

- Would purchase your new service
- Want certain features
- Are willing to pay a certain price
- Prefer certain delivery locations and marketing approaches

There are a variety of ways to collect this information: telephone interviews, mail surveys, face-to-face interviews at schools and businesses, and written or verbal interviews at professional conferences or workshops. Go to wherever your target market congregates, preferably a place where they can spend a few minutes talking to you. For time and cost efficiency, as well as confidentiality, telephone interviews are most often recommended for quantitative data collection.

There is both an art and a science to conducting qualitative and quantitative marketing research. I suggest that you obtain a basic text on marketing research before embarking on this step on your own.

Going to School on the Competition

There are two types of competition you need to study: direct and indirect. A direct competitor offers very similar services to yours and is perceived by prospective buyers as having parallel or equivalent services. An indirect competitor is a person, place, or thing that is very different from your program but that people use instead of your service to derive the same benefits. For example, who would you say are the biggest competitors to your brief-therapy services? Your direct competitors would be all the therapists within a five-to-twenty-mile radius who provide these same services. Your indirect competitors are the places or sources people turn to for help instead of to you: self-help books, videos, magazine articles, EAP offices, ministers, or friends. You can see that there are many more *indirect* competitors taking business away from you than there are direct competitors.

If you study your direct and indirect competitors very carefully, you can often turn some competitors into referral sources. You do this by differentiating and fine-tuning the needs that your services meet in comparison to what the competitors offer. For example, say five competitors in your neighborhood also do brief therapy. You do your homework and find out that none of the five offer weekend crisis services. You decide this is a gap you want to fill. You then meet with each of your "competitors" to see if they would be interested in utilizing this new service. By finding ways to turn competitors into partners and colleagues, you are beginning the very important process of carving out a niche for yourself and establishing a path for long-term survival.

The first thing to look for is a gap in competitors' capabilities or services which you could fill or do better, thereby differentiating yourself from them. Create a profile on every major direct competitor in your area by obtaining a description of all of the following:

1. Geographic area served.
2. Programs offered to each consumer population.
3. Service strengths and capabilities (for example, twenty-four-hour access, convenient location).
4. Staff qualifications and areas of special expertise (for example, multilingual staff).
5. Fees: regular, discount programs, package pricing.
6. Financial backing: do they have sufficient operating capital and reserves to carry them through turbulent times?
7. Reputation among different target audiences. Which programs are known to be doing well? Which are weak?
8. Major referral sources. Where does 80 percent of the competitor's business come from now? Which target groups have they not successfully tapped yet?
9. Major marketing strategies. What is working for them? What are they spending? What are they not doing, either because they haven't tried it or they tried and it didn't work?
10. Overall strengths. What has made them successful?
11. Overall weaknesses. Where do you see them as vulnerable in terms of operations, finances, staff, or marketing?

Then define your competitive response. For each major competitor, write down all the opportunities to differentiate yourself, or to improve upon their services and marketing activities.

Where Do You Get Competitive Information?

The three best sources of competitive information are (1) the competitors themselves (provider, business manager, or CEO), (2) the competitor's old and current clients, and (3) employees who previously worked for the competitor. Each group has a very different perspective on the competitor's organization—and valuable information to share. It is better to collect more information about a few major competitors than to collect a little information about a lot of competitors.

Competitors will meet with you and share a lot of information if you approach them and say, "I would like to discuss how we might differentiate our services and become referral sources, rather than competitors. I would like to meet with you to learn more about what you do and what specialized services you offer which I might refer clients to."

Depending on how competitive or cutthroat your market is, competitors may respond to this approach somewhat skeptically. After you have had a chance to demonstrate that your objective is truly to build a cooperative relationship, you can slowly build trust and open communication. This means you may need to meet more than once. It's important to emphasize here that during an era of vertical and horizontal integration in business, exploring networking and partnering opportunities with a few major competitors is one of the smartest business strategies to follow.

Old and current clients are the richest source of information about what competitors are doing well and what they are not doing well. Ask any dissatisfied customer what a provider did to lose a contract, and they are likely to tell you everything vehemently and in detail. Conversely, satisfied customers will be glad to tell you why they are loyal and won't switch, or under what circumstances they would change.

With clinical customers currently seeking help from your competitors, it would, of course, be unethical to approach them about switching. However, you are competing against other provider groups for *contracting* purposes; thus gathering information about purchaser satisfaction with providers whom they have used previously, or are considering using, is not only ethical but also good business practice.

There are plenty of opportunities to get information from purchaser groups. If, for example, a managed care panel is full and is using your competitors instead of you, you should be actively pursuing relationships with them and meeting with decision makers formally or informally, monthly or bimonthly. During these meetings, ask about generic provider practices that they are satisfied and dissatisfied with.

Then, if you find out through industry or local newspapers or through the grapevine that one of the competitors you've been developing a relationship with recently won a large contract, take a colleague from this organization out to lunch and get all the details. For the modest expense involved, paying for someone's lunch is one of the most effective information-gathering tools in marketing! Be sure to set an appointment as soon as you learn about a change. By having an established relationship, you will have an inside track for getting on the panel if it opens.

Additionally, if you are prospecting (calling leads you don't have a relationship with) and find out that someone is working with a competitor provider group, be sure to ask, "Why was this provider selected? Are they delivering on their promises? What do you wish they did better? Under what circumstances would you consider switching?"

When you are competing for contracts against large group practices, integrated delivery systems, and corporations, then you need to focus on individuals who previously worked for these competitors. They also have a wealth of information to share and will probably give you the most in-depth picture of the organization's internal operations and organizational strengths and weaknesses (financial, marketing, staff, etc.). But keep in mind when interviewing ex-employees that some may have an ax to grind and therefore present the organization more negatively than it actually is. Even so, it's just as likely there is some truth in what they have to say, so listen carefully and then verify important information from other sources. Again, use the invitation-to-lunch technique. Your reason for having a meeting? The ex-employee could be looking for a job, and you may need a new employee or have a job lead once you know more about his or her skills.

You can also gather useful competitive data from written materials and industry information. At local, regional, or national conferences, be sure to pick up competitors' brochures and chat with sales representatives stationed at their booths.

If you are competing for government funding, you can get copies of competitors' proposals submitted to the government under the Freedom of Information Act. For example, in Florida the government put out a request for proposals for a capitated behavioral healthcare program. Many major HMOs and behavioral healthcare MCOs responded. Due to some problems with the RFP, the project had to be rebid. The second time around, the Freedom of Information Act meant every player had access to the other RFPs submitted. You can imagine what the availability of this information did to level the playing field in terms of competitive pricing and services on the second go-round!

Be sure to attend at least one national industry conference a year to learn from industry leaders and competitors who are outside your market area. They can share success and failure stories with you. The Portola Valley, California–based Institute for Behavioral Healthcare's (IBH) annual conference, Behavioral Healthcare *Tomorrow,* is excellent. IBH has also begun holding regional meetings for progressive group practices and networks. These draw a very homogeneous audience, which results in many of the attendees sharing information on common issues.

Usually the most valuable information gathered at industry meetings is from informal conversations taking place between attendees during lunches, receptions, and before and after workshop sessions. As one colleague aptly said, " The measure of a good conference is how much business is done in the halls." Use these opportunities to develop a national network of colleagues who will share information and provide support to each other.

Intelligence Gathering

The other major reason to study your competition intensively is to learn from their experience—both their successes and their failures. Most small and large organizations launching new marketing services or trying to educate the market to buy a new product go through similar developmental stages and make similar mistakes. Study peers, groups, and companies who are a year or more ahead of you in selling similar services. What can you find out about marketing strategies that succeeded or failed? What business growth mistakes did they make and have to correct?

Use the following list as a guide for probing where competitors made the right strategic moves or the wrong ones:

- Did the new program successfully meet a recognized need of a specific target market?
- Is it in a growing market?
- Was it priced correctly?
- Is it easily accessible to customers?
- Does it have sufficient built-in profit margins?
- Was it promoted correctly?
- Does it have solid operations?
- Is there a strong product leader or champion for this new service, and does the organization support and understand the benefits of this new service?
- Is it delivered to the right locations?
- Does it have solid financial backing?

Step 3: Determine what the market will pay for your services.

You have made a lot of progress. You now know the market has a need for your services. You have learned a tremendous amount from your competitors and know which operational and marketing strategies you want to implement based on competitors' experiences. Before you launch your new product, you need to get your financial and business projections in place.

Setting the Price

The best way to set price is to start with what consumers are paying for competitive services. You should have this information from your competitive information gathering. Typically in behavioral healthcare, you will find there is a fairly narrow range of prices paid for a particular service. Your price should fall within this range.

Deciding whether to price your services at the high or low end of a range depends on a number of factors, all related to demand for the new service:

- Demand
- Competition
- Amount of shopping customers do
- Unique features and selling points

Demand and Competition. If there is high demand and little supply, you can easily price at the high end of the price range. Think of popcorn at the movie theater. It costs literally pennies to make, yet theaters charge between two and four dollars for various-sized servings. How can they get away with charging these outrageous prices? Basically, they can charge this much because people will pay it. Consumers have grown accustomed to hot, buttery popcorn when they see a movie and are willing to pay a premium because there is not an alternative supplier or competitor in the theater.

The more competition there is, and the more the supply of services, the more the demand is currently being met and therefore the lower the price. In other words, the greater the number of competitors, the more people will price-shop and place pressure on suppliers to lower prices.

Amount of Shopping Customers Will Do. Historically in healthcare, consumers went to those specialists their primary physicians referred them to. They generally didn't check prices, credentials, or services. This is rapidly changing. Now, consumers who have HMOs, PPOs, or full-choice plans ask practitioners about their fees and credentials before blindly following through on a referral.

In behavioral healthcare, an MCO or EAP usually gives a client three refer-rals to choose from. Therefore, if half or more of a payment is coming out of the consumer's pocket, even pricing your services a little lower (5–10 percent lower) may result in increased referrals. Test it out. The time to price in the lower range is when a reduced price will result in a dramatic increase in referrals. Conversely, if you decide to price the same as or higher than your competitors, be sure you can justify these fees with value-added services.

Unique Selling Points. People will pay more for services, or choose one provider over another, if they believe the selected provider's services are superior in some way. Adding unique points of difference to your products that customers perceive as valuable is a way to keep your services competitive and priced at the higher range. This extra revenue can also, over the long run, provide you with the fi-nancial cushion to keep your services on the cutting edge.

Estimating Demand

How many customers do you think will purchase your services in the next year based on the price you set? This is called estimating demand. Simply take the total number of customers in a target market and estimate that a small percentage (10–20 percent) will buy your services in the first year. For example, if you wish to establish a twenty-four-hour mobile crisis service to meet the psychiatric needs of five local area emergency rooms, you would want to find out the number of psychiatric crisis situations each hospital ER has in an average month. Say this number is ten. This means that there are fifty potential "sales" in a typical month. Since there is at least one competitive service offered by an area psychiatric hos-pital, and your intelligence gathering revealed that it gets twenty calls per month, you can conservatively estimate your initial share of the market to be five to ten monthly referrals, or about 10–20 percent.

You now have the information to estimate how much money you will make in the first year with this new service, and what type of organization you will need to set up to support predicted sales. From this information, you can create a pro forma, which is a financial statement of operations and expected revenue for a new service. The pro forma is a critical tool to help you make a go/no go decision and to predict cash flow if you make a "go" decision.

Step 4: Making a go/no go decision.

It is actually at this point, when you have all the financial costs on paper along with expected revenue, that you can make an objective evaluation as to whether or not offering this new service is a good business decision. For many behavioral healthcare services where profit margins are tight, such as workshops and psychoeducational groups offered to consumers, volume is critical to making a service profitable. Therefore, you may decide the marketing effort and dollars needed to generate the required volume from consumers may not be worth the time involved. Instead, you may choose to market these same services to employers, not to consumers, and spend marketing dollars generating a few big accounts that will result in the desired volume and revenue.

There are other factors to consider in addition to the financial ones when making a go/no go decision. For example, you may need to provide a new service to complete your continuum of care or to strengthen your competitive position, even though the new service may only break even or lose a small amount of money.

In making the go/no go decision, new services under consideration should be reviewed carefully according to the criteria in the New Product Evaluation form (Exhibit 4.1 in the Appendix, designed to be photocopied for your use).

If you want to formalize this evaluation process further, you can weigh each variable according to its importance to your organization. This will give you a more finely tuned analysis of the pros and cons of the new service.

Step 5: Pilot your service.

Congratulations; you have made a "go" decision on your new service. Are you ready to market it yet? No. You *still* have a few more steps before that.

The next critical step is piloting your new service. This means trying it out on a small group of customers. The purpose of this step is to get the bugs out of the delivery of the service, and to make sure you have a strong product that accomplishes what it sets out to accomplish. Test-running your project also allows you to make mistakes on a small scale and not risk losing a big account. Therefore it is often advantageous when recruiting pilot customers to be very open and say you are testing a new service. Explain ahead of time that system and delivery problems will probably occur. Encourage your pilot customers to provide a lot of feedback and to help shape the new service. In exchange for their patience and assistance, customers using a service in the pilot phase typically get a reduced rate. By using this approach you involve clients in creating a successful service— a very effective strategy!

While operations staff are fine-tuning and test-running the new service, this is a good time to develop a formal marketing plan and sales strategy. The next chapter helps you do this.

CHAPTER FIVE

DEVELOPING A MARKETING PLAN AND STEPS TO SUCCESSFUL SALES

Dee Pearce

To be successful in the managed care environment you must prepare for your sales effort by making a marketing plan before you start selling. Just as your success in treating a patient depends on the completeness and accuracy of your diagnosis and treatment plan, the success of your sales effort is directly dependent on the completeness and accuracy of your marketing diagnostics and planning.

Before you start selling, you need to sit down and ask yourself a number of key questions. The first and most important diagnostic question is: "Who is my customer?" In other words, "Who is shopping for, needs to use, and can buy my program or service?" The Customer Form ("Who Is My Customer?") in the Appendix helps you identify all of your customers. If you can answer the questions in the form, you are well on your way to a solid marketing plan. (The blank Customer Form, Exhibit 5.1 in the Appendix, is meant to be photocopied for your own use.)

Who Is My Customer?

In identifying who your customer is, the first concept that you must grasp is that the person who eventually *uses* your service is often *not* the person who *shops* for the services, who *pays* for the services, or who *decides* what services are purchased.

In fact, if you are trying to market your practice to a large organization like an insurance carrier or integrated health system, each of those roles is likely to be played by a different person. All of these people are your customers. Just as each patient has a unique treatment plan that you devise after a complete diagnosis, so too must you look at the unique needs of the people in each of these roles and learn how to market (sell) to each according to his or her needs.

Being successful at marketing and sales in the managed care environment is a lot like stir-fry cooking, because the chef spends a lot of time slicing and dicing the elements of the dish being prepared, but when all is ready the dish takes just moments to cook. The more marketing homework you do up front, the more business you will obtain without wasting a lot of time chasing "unqualified" prospective customers.

Imagine a ten-person practice that includes psychiatrists, psychologists, nurse practitioners, and licensed professional counselors. The group's specialty is child and adolescent mental health, with special expertise in eating disorders. The group wants to increase its practice.

They hope to

- Provide services for individual clients
- Contract with local PPOs to be a preferred provider
- Provide their program and services to referrers from
  The school system
  The courts
  The county
- Attract referrals
  From inpatient services
  From other colleagues, and so forth

Each of the potential purchasers or referrers represents a market segment that shops and buys differently. You need to know how to pursue or target each of those segments. The concept of *target marketing* is based on the same concept as any other kind of targeting: you will not hit anything unless you aim for it. In surgery, you won't be able to find that septic gall bladder unless you aim for it. It's the same thing in marketing: you must know exactly where and how to look for each kind of customer. Believe me, the way professionals in an integrated healthcare system shop and contract for services is very different from how an individual patient shops.

To illustrate use of The Customer Form (Exhibit 5.1 in the Appendix) in targeting a market segment, we will assume just one target: the parents of adolescents with eating disorders. I have filled in an example of the Customer Form for you (Exhibit 5.1 here), using the imaginary ten-person practice.

EXHIBIT 5.1. SAMPLE OF COMPLETED CUSTOMER FORM.

Who Is My Customer?

Example: Targeting the Parents of Adolescents with Eating Disorders

Questions about the targeted group	*Answers about the targeted group*
Is the person who will be the eventual user (the *end user*) of your program or service the same person who shops for it (the *shopper*)?	*Who is the end user?* The eventual user is an adolescent.
	Who is the shopper? The shopper is the parent, or guardian.
Is the person who shops for the service (the *shopper*) the same person that the purchaser will seek out for expert advice (the *expert advisor*)?	*Who is the expert advisor?* The family pediatrician or other medical provider is likely to be the "expert" that the shopping parent will turn to. Other experts might include friends who have had children who needed similar help, school counselors, and ministers.
Who will be the final decision maker (the *decision maker*) on what will or can be bought?	*Who is the decision maker?* The decision maker will be the person who holds the purse strings or has some legal authority. This could be the parent, the insurance carrier, or another authority that will pay for the service.
Who actually pays for the service? The person who writes the check is the *guarantor*.	*Who is the guarantor?* The parents, if they are paying out of pocket; otherwise, an insurance carrier or agency.

The Psychological Profile of the Customer

Does the same person fill each of the following roles? If not, what do the people in each of these roles *need, want, and value?*

- End user
- Shopper
- Expert advisor
- Decision maker
- Guarantor

Construct a psychological profile of each of these key customers by answering the questions that follow.

(Fill in a separate form for each kind of customer: the end user of your service, the shopper, the expert advisor, the decision maker, and the guarantor.)

What does the customer hope will happen if their needs are met? (The answers to this and the next question identify the customer's needs. This helps you define what should go into your product/service.)

EXHIBIT 5.1. SAMPLE OF COMPLETED CUSTOMER FORM, cont'd.

Parents hope that their child will stop the self-abuse. They hope that there is a medical solution. They hope they can find the right people to help. They hope they can afford professional care. They hope that a solution is accessible to them.

What does the customer fear will happen if their needs are not met? (The answer to this question will give you additional information about the sense of urgency of the client and information about their specific needs for service.)
Parents fear that their child will die. They fear that they cannot stop it. They fear the embarrassment of the situation. They fear they will be blamed.

Why are they shopping at this time? How urgent is their need? (You will find some customer segments, for example, the PPOs, who may not have a perceived urgent need. If you want their business, you will either have to be very persistent or create a sense of urgency with them.)
The child is becoming increasingly sick. The need is urgent.

What have they been doing to meet this need until now? (This identifies the customer's perceived alternatives. These alternatives may be competitors. Or you may be able to partner with the competitors in a way that works for both of you and ends up generating referrals for you. In either case, you need to know who they are.)
They have been taking the child to their pediatrician.

Do they already have experience with your sort of service? Do they have a prior relationship with another provider of this service? (This identifies how much educating you have to do as part of your marketing the unique value of your service. It also identifies whether they have potential loyalty to another provider.)
No, they have never used any psychiatric services.

If so, what have they valued and what have they wanted to change about the prior relationship(s)? (The answer to this question tells you what it will take for your service to attract these potential clients away from what they are now using.)
They have never used any counseling or psychiatric services. Psychiatric services have negative connotations.

What do they see as the alternatives they can use to solve their needs?
They hope to continue to use the nonpsychiatric physician—their pediatrician or internist.

What is their perception about you, your organization, and your service?
They don't know anything about you except what they have heard from their expert advisor. In general they believe that psychiatric care is for crazy people or weak-willed losers. They don't want to be associated with a psychiatric provider.

How to Use the Information to Plan Your Marketing and Product Offering

All of the factors listed in The Customer Form contribute to the buying decision. If instead of the teenager's parent your target customer is a county government agency, a PPO, or a medical colleague, you simply get different answers to the same questions.

The answers tell you where and how your target customer shops and who will be making the decisions. To market successfully, you have to be known by the shopper, or by the person who is the expert advisor to the shopper. In the example of the ten-person practice, you would need to be known by local pediatricians, internists, school counselors, and ministers. How do you accomplish this? You can arrange to give a speaking engagement, make cards or brochures for their offices, or simply introduce yourself and leave a card.

The answers to these questions also give you a better idea of what your product ought to include. Here, the psychological profile tells you that the customer identified as the adolescent's parent has a higher sense of trust and comfort with nonpsychiatric medicine. So you might consider bringing a pediatrician or an internist into the practice group both to give the program medical expertise and to defuse the psychiatric image of the practice.

As you fill in the form, remember that you must address the needs and concerns of each person who plays a role: shopper, expert advisor, decision maker, guarantor, and end user. You must market to all of them.

Make a number of copies of the form, and fill one out for each of your target groups: fill one out with the county in mind, one for the schools, the PPOs, medical colleagues, etc.

You would get different answers if you were to envision targeting an insurance company. The fact is, in using this form you will find that each market segment has very different needs. Identifying these needs helps you refine the features of services you are offering; the process points directly to the best ways to find and market to your customers.

Writing a Marketing and Sales Plan

After you know who your customer is, you can write a marketing and sales plan. This plan is a tool to use what you know about your customer to plan how to achieve a targeted level of sales in the coming year.

Exhibit 5.2 is a filled-in sample of the basic Marketing and Sales Plan found in the Appendix. It shows how a finished plan would look. You are encouraged

EXHIBIT 5.2. SAMPLE OF
COMPLETED BASIC MARKETING AND SALES PLAN.

I. Executive Overview

The executive overview gives a capsule presentation of your marketing and sales strategy and plans for the next fiscal year.

In the next year the practice will be challenged by a 30 percent increase in the number of psychiatric providers for adolescents in the immediate area.

However, we believe that we will be able to achieve our marketing and sales targets because
   - The competition is new, unknown, and without a specific product or niche.
   - We will be emphasizing our position as the only full-service provider in the region for adolescents with eating disorders.
   - We have identified the key purchasers of these services in the region.
   - Those responsible for meeting the sales targets will be trained in the consultative sales process.
   - For the first time, each month we will track our sales activities (the time spent for identifying customers, the number of presentations we have made, etc.), analyze the results of our sales work vis-à-vis our sales targets, and make appropriate adjustments to the monthly focus of our sales activities.
   - We will be standardizing our product/service offerings so that we can also standardize our prices.

II. Major Challenges Facing the Organization in the Coming Year

A. Competition

A new four-person pediatric and adolescent behavioral medicine practice group has located adjacent to the local medical center. This is a 30 percent increase in the number of providers of adolescent psychiatry within a thirty-minute drive.

B. Strengths, weaknesses, opportunities, threats ("SWOT" analysis)
   - Strengths: reputation, location
   - Weaknesses: lack of standardized products and services; lack of focus on and periodic analysis of the most productive sales activities to enable us to make our sales targets
   - Opportunities: joint ventures
   - Threats: new state regulations and new competitor entrant

III. Review of Last Year's Marketing Efforts: What Worked, What Didn't, and Why
   - Referral development works.
   - Shotgunning efforts did not work.

IV. Major Objectives and Directions the Organization Plans to Take in the Coming Year
   - Products
   - Establish standard products
   - Establish standard bundling of services
   - Pricing: reevaluate the payment schedule
   - Positioning: establish a unique niche for our services
   - Sales operations: train personnel; establish periodic evaluation of sales activities vis-à-vis success at achieving sales goals

V. Brief Description of New Products/Services and Product Updates (If You Can't Articulate It, You Can't Sell It)

An intensive outpatient service for adolescents with eating disorders:
   - A 12-week-long program

EXHIBIT 5.2. SAMPLE OF
COMPLETED BASIC MARKETING AND SALES PLAN, cont'd.

- Clients attend three times per week after school hours—two evenings and one weekend day for up to four hours each, for a combination of
  - Group and individual therapies
  - Case management
  - Medical monitoring, including lab work and medication as indicated

VI. Sales Objective for the Next Fiscal Year; Strategies to Accomplish Objectives (Do a Few Things Well!)

    A. Develop and close contracts with the following target groups:
  - Managed care organizations
  - Child and family services
  - School systems

    B. Target sales goal, by customer group for the next fiscal year

Targeted Groups for Next Fiscal Year	Number of Members/ Potential Clients*	Estimated Sales Goal (Dollars)**
Managed care organizations 10 MCOs	40,000 Adolescent members/ 400 Potential clients	$240,000.00
Child and family services 6 Agencies	30,000 Adolescent members/ 300 Potential clients	$180,000.00
Existing customers (parents)	200 Current clients/ 50 Referrals	$30,000.00
School systems 20 Systems	20,000 Adolescents/ 200 Potential clients	$120,000.00
Totals	950 Potential clients	$570,000.00

*Number of potential clients is based on an estimate that 10/1,000 adolescents will receive help through our practice.

**Estimated revenue per client is calculated at an average of eight outpatient sessions at $75.00 per session ($600.00 per case).

    C. Major strategies to accomplish objective VI.A.:
  - Identify key contact people
  - Qualify potential customers
  - Set up presentations
  - Monthly, evaluate sales activities vis-à-vis meeting sales targets, and adjust the focus of the activities

VII. Sales Implementation Plan by Month or Quarter

    A. Quantifiable sales goals (should be stretch goals but achievable)
  - Close 3–5 new contracts per quarter
  - Identify and qualify 25 new leads per month
  - Make 5 presentations
  - Submit 2–4 contract proposals per month
  - Review and analyze sales progress vis-à-vis goals each month; adjust focus and activities accordingly

EXHIBIT 5.2. SAMPLE OF
COMPLETED BASIC MARKETING AND SALES PLAN, cont'd.

B. Identifying prospective customers: prospecting
    - Reserve one morning and one afternoon each week for prospecting
    - Make and log a minimum of 10 prospecting calls each week
C. Promoting the practice (refer to Chapter Eight, "Promoting Your Services")
    - Attend three regional and one national conferences sponsored by target groups
    - Speaking engagements: make at least one public presentation per quarter
    - Visits or calls to referral sources: schedule a minimum of one afternoon per month to talk to potential referral sources
    - Other public relations: talk to appropriate editors of local papers and professional journals; find out what they want for articles; submit articles and press releases, minimum of two articles and four press releases in the next year
    - Evaluate and monitor conformance with this plan at least once every quarter (schedule it)
D. Advertising (list what you plan to do, by type of advertising)
    - Investigate efficacy of radio spots targeted to the commute hour to reach parents of adolescents with eating disorders, plus other potential referral sources
    - Investigate possibility of buying space in local professional newsletters for referrers, for example, pediatricians, ministers, school counselors
E. Sales materials (use sales collateral materials to reinforce positioning)
    - Be consistent with positioning statements in text of all marketing materials
    - Make reprints of published articles and press clippings
    - Develop generic (boilerplate) contract materials, presentation materials, and proposals
    - Develop trifold brochures describing the eating disorders program that can be handed out or put in a stand-up display in a pediatrician's office,or sent to local potential referrers such as ministers and school counselors
F. Budget (develop a marketing budget, by activity, for example, the cost of traveling to conferences, and the cost of sales collaterals. Develop a sales budget—both the cost of personnel and the cost of operations.)
    Marketing expenses
    - Conferences
    - Sales collaterals
    - Marketing planning
    Sales expenses
    - Personnel
    - Transportation
    - Food and lodging
    - Phone, mail, and photocopies

to photocopy the blank Marketing and Sales Plan form in the Appendix for your own use.

The Fundamentals of How to Sell in the Managed Care Environment–No Matter What Product or Service You Are Offering

If you are simply trying to increase the number and sources of referrals to your practice group, or if you are trying to develop a business relationship between yourself and a large integrated healthcare service, sooner or later you are going to end up selling.

Selling. The very idea is off-putting to most clinicians. Clinicians tend to think of selling as something slightly smarmy and lowdown. To be successful in selling, you have to let go of that preconception. Let me help.

You are not going to be doing anything that is unethical, "in your face," or even the slightest bit obnoxious or off-putting. You say you don't have a sales personality? You do not need chutzpah—you don't even have to be an extrovert— if you have done your marketing and sales planning homework. Instead, you are simply using your best diagnostic skills. You are not selling anybody on anything. You are helping people meet their needs—in fact, many people who have specific and urgent needs, and who value your service.

At some time in your past, you were urgently shopping for something. You weren't sure exactly where to go to find what you needed, but when you found a source, you wanted to be sure that the item or service would meet your needs and that you were making a good, informed decision.

Consultative sales provides such answers. A consultative sale is analogous to diagnosis, treatment, and follow-up. There is a specific process that all effective consultative salespersons are aware of and work through. It is known as the *sales cycle*, and it amounts to the steps that must be taken in every sale. In its most straightforward form, the sales cycle consists of six steps:

- Generating leads
- Qualifying
- Presenting
- Answering objections
- Closing
- Servicing

To obtain and maintain contracts and clients, you or somebody who works with you has to carry out each step. I have listed them in the order in which they usually occur.

The most effective salespersons raise their ability to accomplish these steps to an art form. If you master and use them in each and every sale, you will be highly productive. If you ignore any one of the steps, you are not likely to succeed. As you read through the descriptions of the steps that follow, you will find that you already use many of the skills required to successfully navigate the sales cycle.

Surprisingly, the most valuable skills are those you use constantly in behavioral therapies: probing for information, active listening, clarifying and reflecting back, and, above all, respecting the client.

If you have done your marketing thoroughly, and you are still having trouble selling, look back at the steps of the sales cycle and examine your work. Chances are that you are not performing one of the steps of the sales cycle well enough, if at all.

One further note before we proceed. Sometimes a sale zips through the sales cycle so quickly that you may not even know you have been through the stages. Conversely, just one stage can take months of painstaking work. You can generally expect that the larger the contract, and the larger the entity you are dealing with, the longer and more complex the process.

Generating Leads

Generating leads is sometimes called "farming" or "prospecting." These terms accurately describe the process, because generating leads can take a long time. As in farming, you sow seeds, cultivate them, and later—but only if the soil is right and the weather favorable—you harvest at the right time. As in prospecting, generating leads is like looking for precious metal. Even if you are a competent geologist, you have to turn over a lot of rocks to identify a body of ore. Both of these analogies hold true about generating leads, but there are ways to become as efficient and effective as possible.

For starters, refer back to your marketing plan. The psychological profile of your customer, which you developed in the Customer Form "Who Is My Customer?" (see Exhibit 5.1 in the Appendix and in this chapter), tells you where to find all of your customers, what their concerns are, and how they shop for services. It tells you who will be shopping for your services, who the person is who needs to use your service, and who has the power to sign up for your service.

Targeting a prospective sales audience is critical. Think about it: you cannot hit a target if you don't aim for it. Yet many salespeople shoot in any old direction and then wonder why their success rate is dismal. (Chapter Three, you will recall, provided detailed guidance for targeting prospective customers in managed care, employer, and physician organizations.)

So, lesson one: target your audience. Use the intelligence you have gleaned from your marketing homework so that you spend your limited resources going after just those prospective purchasers who *already* want and need your services.

Do not let yourself be deluded by beginner's grandiosity, which says, "Well, so and so should want . . . really ought to be using . . . my service; if I can only get in front of them, I'm sure I could sell them on the idea." It's a major temptation, but forget it. You only want to spend your time talking to prospective purchasers who already know that they want and need the kind of service that you offer.

Lead generation is the single most daunting part of sales for most beginning salespersons. It involves personally getting in touch with an individual you have identified as a prospective shopper for, referrer to, or buyer of your kind of service. The key word is *personally*. For starters, you must know the person's name, since you must get in touch with him or her directly. Not his or her secretary, not the department, not the organization. The person.

Step one is to get the shopper or buyer's name. How? Call and ask. Let others help you. When you call, simply ask the person who answers the telephone to help you find the name of the person responsible for shopping for or deciding to buy your kind of service. When you have the name, call and ask for him or her directly.

You must be prepared to (1) give a message to anyone else who answers the phone and (2) introduce yourself and the reason for your call. This is done best if you spend some time thinking it out in advance, practicing out loud, and writing down what you want to say—in a sentence or two, maximum. Your message must be directed to benefit, or in some definite way help out, the shopper.

"Hello Mr. Richards? My name is Dee Pearce. Are you the person who is responsible for contracting for mental health services for adolescents with eating disorders?" If the answer is yes, continue. If no, ask if he or she could tell you who that person is, or refer you to a person who would know.

If the person you are talking to is conversational and sounds informed, you can ask what he or she knows about how decisions are made in contracting for mental health services for adolescents. Getting this information tells you if contracting for your kind of service is a multifaceted process, who is involved in the decision-making process, if it is done only at a certain time of year, and so forth.

Assuming the answer is yes, that this is the person who contracts for adolescent services; then continue. "I'm calling to let you know that The Family Practice in Berkeley [or the entity you represent] offers an eating disorder service for adolescents. Is that type of service something you are looking for at this time?"

If yes, proceed to qualifying (the next step in the sales cycle). If no, ask: "Do you anticipate looking for those services any time in the future?" If yes, ask for elaboration. You may even partially get into qualifying, by asking if he or she would like you to send some information on your service. Ask when it would be most appropriate to call back at a time when he or she will be shopping for these services.

Did you notice that everything you have said has been potentially helpful to the person? You have given information that there is a service source he or she may not have known about. You are offering to get back in touch when he or she needs to know about your kind of service.

You may also have noticed that I have not mentioned sending a letter or materials in advance of your first personal contact. Sending materials or a letter in advance is an extra step, and not a very useful one. Remember, until you have talked to the prospective shopper, you don't even know if you are addressing the right person. The chances of someone seeing your letter, and then taking the time to figure out who it should be passed on to, and then actually passing it along are practically zero. As for a direct mail campaign (which is what you are doing by mailing ahead, even to a carefully targeted audience), if you are an unknown entity your mailing will typically have a response rate of less than one percent. Even if your letter does get to the right person, don't expect your letter to be so compelling that this person will pick up the phone to call you. That is pure wishful thinking. It may happen once in a blue moon, but you are going to miss most of your potential business because the chances are so slight that someone is in the market for your services right at the time you send a letter. And if they're not shopping now but will be shopping in the future, you'll never know that if you don't call!

Some people believe that introducing themselves in advance by mail is more polite, less pushy. Not so. You have just sent another stack of materials to someone who has to shuffle it around. In fact, a quick and polite "Are you shopping?" on the phone is much more courteous. So save printing material and postage. Pick up the phone and call. You'll be glad you did because you will know firsthand where you stand. By calling, you have authoritative (and current) information about whether and when to proceed with this potential client. You now have a list of people who are actively seeking knowledge about your kind of service.

When the person you have called says he or she is ready to shop, the next step is to qualify the person.

Qualifying

Your clinical training predisposes you to do an excellent job of qualifying a prospective purchaser: it's just like doing a complete intake and evaluation on a patient. You need to know the prospect's complete history, along with presenting complaints or conditions. As in the diagnostic process, if you miss any vital information you could end up heading down a nonproductive path.

Here is a list of basic questions that you want answered by the time you finish qualifying the person. They fall into several diagnostic categories:

- Needs analysis—both wants and aversions
- The perspective client's previous experience with a similar product or service
- The sense of urgency
- The decision-making process
- Who the decision makers are
- The needs and agendas of each of the decision makers
- Any other agendas

In my role as vice president of business development in a national healthcare company, I found the questions in The Qualifying Interview Form (Exhibit 5.3 in the Appendix) to be a highly effective set of tools, when used properly. You may find it useful to convert this set of questions into a standard interview form that you fill out during or immediately after the qualifying interview. Capturing the questions on a form reminds you graphically of any pieces of information that are still missing. This is crucial, because lack of any key piece of information may cause you to make false assumptions and head off unproductively.

Begin the qualifying interview with a preview of what you want to ask. Frame it in a way that highlights the client's interest, something like this:

> Ms. Jefferson, if it's OK with you, I'd like to ask you just a couple of questions to make certain that the service we offer fits your needs. If it doesn't, I'll do my best to refer you to other sources. If it appears that what we provide is a good fit, I'd like to know a few things about your plans and your selection process. This will help us to provide you with just the information that will be most useful to you, when you want it. Does that sound OK?

I have never had anyone refuse this chance to talk about their wants, desires, needs, and frustrations. Even if there is not a fit, you get high marks and future referrals to your service from this person should you refer them on. But if it looks as though it may be a match, say so simply: "It looks like we may be able to help. I'd like to ask you just a couple more questions, if I may."

At this point, when you see that what you have to offer is really appropriate for them, you might be powerfully tempted to start right in telling them about your offering. You must resist this temptation; it will be perceived as "selling," and you still need a lot more information. It is most important now that you attend to your potential client's perceptions. Doing so builds trust that you are not going to be a pushy salesperson and demonstrates that you are honestly interested in their needs. You are then able to find out a great deal more about their situation and whether you should be pursuing this client.

Getting answers to *all* the questions in the interview form lets you know right away whether and when there might be business for you. If you miss getting information on *any* of these topics, you could spend years chasing business that will never materialize for you. I have seen it happen. There are some common barriers to sales that the salesperson fails to uncover, such as

- This is just a routine comparative shopping venture and there is little likelihood of any change.
- The shopper is interested but does not have the authority to buy, and the person who has the final approval isn't shopping at all.
- There is no sense of urgency.
- The decision has to pass a county commission and a state budget process.
- The people involved want to create their own service and just want to know, by way of talking to you, what is out there.

Thorough qualifying can save you months or years of work!

When you have the answers to *all* the questions, you are in a position to decide whether or not this is a real candidate for your pipeline, or whether to put them in a tickler file to call a year from now, or whether to simply bow out.

For people who are working hard to get new business, the hardest thing to know is, as any great card player can tell you, "when to hold them." I have seen hundreds of man-hours and thousands of travel dollars and other expenses invested in a poorly qualified prospect. It is magical thinking to believe you are going to sell to people when they don't want to buy or are not really in a position to buy. If you want to close business, qualify, qualify, qualify. Have you noticed that we haven't started "selling" yet?

Filling Out the Qualifying Interview Form. The questions in the Qualifying Interview Form (Exhibit 5.3 in the Appendix, to be photocopied for your use) are very generic. This is deliberate. Exactly as with probing questions in diagnostics, in qualifying you want to direct the questioning without leading the client or limiting the answers. I encourage you to add other probing questions, based on your experiences over time.

It's unlikely that your initial contact will be able to supply you with all of this information, especially the vital details of the unique interests and prejudices of each person involved in the decision-making process. You must talk to all the participants. Take the lead in this. Tell your contact that you will best be able to address his or her interests if you talk to each of the people involved. Ask your contact person to help you get in touch with each of the decision makers.

Qualify each decision maker—individually. You can check each person's perception of his or her needs and the buying process. You will get very different views, but in the end you'll have an overall view of what the issues, agenda, and process of selecting and purchasing are.

If your contact is a lower-ranking person and the real decision is to be made higher up, ask to speak with the highest-level decision maker. Tell your contact that in order for you to best address the organization's needs, it's important to make sure that you completely understand what the top person is looking for and wants to accomplish. Ask the contact to arrange for the two of you to have ten minutes with the top decision maker. If the top decision maker is in earnest about this search, he or she will almost certainly give you a few minutes to share his or her viewpoint. When you meet (the best way) or conference call (a fallback option) with the decision maker, reiterate what your contact has told you about their needs and process, and ask if there is anything further or different that he or she wants you to understand about either the organization's needs or process. Then listen, carefully. When the decision maker finishes talking, ask how he or she wants you to continue to work with them. You want to know if your initial contact is the person who will be spearheading this review or if you should be working with someone else. Thank the decision maker and your initial contact. Do *not* sell or present your services.

This meeting is critical. When you finish you will know what the important issues are and whether there really is an intent to secure an agreement for your kind of service.

Requests for Proposals (RFPs) and Requests for Information (RFIs). A word about Requests for Proposals and Information. These days, if you are a known provider of services and the entity that is shopping for services knows of you already, along with other potential providers you will receive an RFI or RFP. The art and science of responding to an RFP deserves its own chapter; here, let us say that one way to become much more competitive in the RFP process is to get in touch with the persons who are issuing the RFP and walk through the qualifying process in advance of answering the RFP. The worst thing you can do is to pull together a pile of boilerplate and/or marketing materials and send them in without knowing the real issues, needs, selection process, and agenda of your potential client. Never assume that the RFP gives all the information you need for a response that speaks to the client's real issues.

Previewing and Setting Parameters. One more thing you need to understand before we go on with the selling part of the sales cycle: as the agent for your service, you are the expert. Just as you would guide a patient through diagnosis and treatment, a responsible and effective salesperson must guide the buyer through the process so that the buyer gets the information and support that he or she needs to make informed decisions. You have already read suggestions for guiding the process in the section on qualifying, where, I recommended that

- You tell the prospective client that you need to ask them certain questions.
- For you to best "treat" them, you must understand their issues fully.
- You let them know that if you can't help them you will refer them to someone who can.

Just as you would in treating a patient, at each stage of the sales process tell the person what you are doing, what you need to know from them, and what you will be doing next. I call this process previewing and setting parameters.

Previewing and setting parameters keeps everybody informed, on track, and sharing common expectations. It allows you and your client to agree on expectations up front, and then for you to meet those expectations successfully. If you do not preview, set, and agree on parameters as you go along, then the prospective client may set and invent all sorts of expectations that you will not be willing or able to meet—or worse yet, that you might not even be aware of.

Presenting

The next step is the presentation. In the presentation, you are the expert, so it is important that you (1) preview for the prospective client what you will be covering in your presentation, (2) check during the presentation to see if they have any questions, and (3) afterward check to make sure your presentation meets their needs for information.

The sales presentation is the forum in which you demonstrate how your offering meets their needs. Please notice that I do not say that this is where you sell your service. You may be justly proud of your offering and its many positive features, but if you only present the features and do not clearly tie those features to issues that are important to the clients, you have not helped the clients see why they should be interested in your offering. This is where the work that you did to qualify your potential clients comes into play.

You prepare for your presentation by listing all of the clients' issues: their needs, wants, and aversions. Then to prepare the body of your presentation, bring in each issue one at a time, use the examples that they gave you in your qualifying interview, and show how your services address each one. The benefits you will talk about in the presentation are not general benefits that you feel that they ought to value, but benefits that address their issues directly.

Following the rule of previewing and setting parameters, begin the actual presentation by telling your audience what you are going to tell them and what will happen next. At the end of every major segment of your presentation, that is, the formal presentation, any demonstration or interactive period, and the question-and-answer period, wrap up by telling them what has just been said and what is coming next. This is called signposting.

It is known that 75 percent of our learning is done visually, with the other 25 percent done kinesthetically (by doing) or aurally (by listening). It is therefore very important that you use visual presentation materials, and distribute handouts of your overheads or slides for people to take notes on. This is a key to your presentation. Your visual materials should receive your careful attention; concentrate on graphical and pictorial illustrations.

If your speech is carefully signposted, and if you provide illustrative presentation materials and individual handouts to be written on during your presentation, then you have covered all the ways that most help your audience assimilate information.

It's a good idea to preface the presentation about your service by introducing yourself and offering your credentials. They include all of the things that make you and your entity a creditable choice. These might be the size and age of your operation, your experience, the number of your clients, and names of clients that your listeners will know personally or respect by reputation. The object is to give those who are considering you a feeling that they are in reputable and respected hands . . . that they will be proud to be in the company of your other clients.

I have often found that it is useful, after presentation of your credentials, to explain that you've talked to each of the attendees; then recap the issues they listed for you in the earlier sessions, and ask for any corrections or additions to the list. It is a nice touch to record these on a flip chart in front of the group. You have already previewed that you are presenting your service and how it can speak to those issues, so ask once more, "Is there anything else that you want to make certain that we address?" Then make certain to do so in the course of your presentation.

The consensus is that the core of a presentation should never be longer than fourteen minutes. This is good advice. If in fourteen minutes you cannot convey to an audience whose issues you know what your service can do to address their issues, then you need to work on your presentation.

Answering Objections

The next piece of your presentation is to answer any outstanding questions. By all means encourage questions, because unanswered questions are objections. Objections are anything in the buyer's mind that causes hesitancy and apprehension about selecting or purchasing your offering. In fact your whole presentation has been designed to address issues, show how your service meets the clients' needs, and solve the problems that they are currently having or that they fear they will have. You have uncovered all of these potential objections in your qualifying interviews, so you are now able to raise each potential question, uncertainty, or fear and answer it.

Along with the outstanding questions, you must take care to address any unasked questions or unspoken hesitations. These may include commonly held negative perceptions about your service, concerns about costs, fear of risk, and others. You must take these head-on and satisfy and reassure your potential clients.

You can do yourself a big favor, before making any presentations, by sitting down and listing all of the objections that you have ever heard about your service. Try to anticipate any hesitancies that your audience might have and prepare to answer them in advance. In spite of your best preparation, of course, more often than not an objection comes flying out of the audience just when you think you have finished giving a marvelous presentation.

One of the most useful techniques I have ever encountered for handling a surprise objection is called the "porcupine." It works like this. Someone throws you a threatening question. Instead of answering it immediately, you throw the prickly question back by asking the questioner to amplify the question or the outcome he or she is concerned about. A simple example:

Questioner: Do you offer services on Saturdays and Sundays?
Response: Why is weekend service important to you?
Questioner: Well it's just that I work, and I want to be able to get service outside of business hours.

Another porcupine response:

Questioner: Are your services accessible?
Response: Accessible in what way?
Questioner: Accessible for electric wheelchairs.

These examples illustrate that you need to get a feel for the magnitude of the objection and what is underlying the question in order to give an appropriate response. Using the porcupine also gives you a moment to collect your thoughts and frame your response. At its core the porcupine is respectful of the concerns and issues of your prospective client while it prevents you from jumping in with a glib but ineffectual answer.

Closing

The presentation ends with a closing statement. In sales, *closing* means the final step to get agreement to do business together. A closing statement is your way of asking for the prospective client's business.

If you are lucky, the client closes for you with a statement such as, "Why don't we get together next week to go over a contract?" In fact you should be closing all the time. Attempting to close is often the only way to know where you stand vis-à-vis any competition, or the process itself, and so forth. Individual styles of closing questions are all over the board. Here a few examples:

- "Is this the kind of program you want?"
- "Do you feel that you are ready to move forward?"
- "Would you like to set up a time to go over a contract?"

Questions like these are designed to elicit any further objections or steps that need to be taken. There is also the assumptive close: "I can have contracts ready by Monday; would that be a good time for you?" I don't want to put words in your mouth. Rather, I hope to impress on you that you must be closing, testing the water on the purchaser's readiness to buy, and looking for any further objections all the time.

There is one thing about closing that you should fix firmly in your mind. *Stop selling when the client says yes!* When the client says, "Yes, I would like to contract for your service," *do not* insist on telling him or her about one more benefit, or that he or she talk to some of your happy clients. Just smile, nod, and do what your customer wants.

Not Closing. Sometimes you will be eliminated as a contender. When this happens, I highly recommend that you run, not walk, back to the prospective client who eliminated. Ask him or her in a kind manner to tell you candidly why your offering was eliminated. This gives you and your company a chance to change your offering, your price, your approach to selling, or whatever is acted as a barrier to consummating this sale and possibly others.

A Reminder and Caution About the Sales Cycle. Even though they claim to have mastered all the steps of the sales cycle, many salespeople still insist that the client must undergo the whole process step by step in order. Let me emphasize that all the steps in the sales cycle vary greatly in duration and intensity from case to case. Generally the lower the costs involved in a purchase decision, and the fewer the decision makers who need to agree on a decision, the shorter the sales cycle. But even this is highly variable from buyer to buyer. It has been known for a prospective client to call up and ask for a salesperson to come over, and then and there calculate the costs of and sign a multimillion dollar, multiyear contract. On the other hand, some people delay making a thousand-dollar contract decision for years, each year asking multiple companies to submit elaborate proposals and travel great distances to make presentations.

The steps of the sales cycle can be compressed into a single phone call, or they can take years. You will be most productive if you learn to collapse the steps of the sales cycle into the smallest time frame possible. If the prospective buyer is qualified and wants to hear about your product and sign a check all in one encounter, do not insist that he have a formal presentation, and so forth. Stop selling. Take the check and say thank you.

Service as Sales

All the work you do to market and sell effectively to prospective clients is useless unless your clients perceive that the service they are receiving meets their needs and is the best value they can get. The key words here are *clients* and *perceive*.

It is often extremely difficult for healthcare providers to understand this concept. As a professional you have been expected to prescribe what's best for the patient. In a competitive environment such as managed care, the client's satisfaction is on a par with clinical outcomes. Therefore one of the most useful things you can do is continue to stay in touch with your clients and regularly ask them what they think about your service:

- What do they value about your service?
- Are you meeting their expectations?
- What do they think you are doing well?
- What would they like you to do differently or better?

Then act on that information! Just having you ask is valued by your clients. Acting to address the issues and values of your clients puts you head and shoulders above your competition.

◆ ◆ ◆

Remember:

- If you do a complete diagnostic marketing evaluation and treatment plan
- If you master the steps of the sales cycle
- If your clients perceive that you serve their needs and provide value

If you do all this, then you will obtain and retain many clients. You will have justly earned them!

CHAPTER SIX

FINDING YOUR PLACE IN THE INTEGRATED DELIVERY SYSTEM

David W. Allen, Jr.

An "integrated delivery system" doesn't sound like a comfortable place for a mental health professional, but it is exactly where therapists with successful and busy practices will be working in the coming years. As a psychiatric medical group administrator and, over the past six years or so, a consultant to behavioral healthcare providers across the country, I know that it is possible for ethical, caring mental health professionals to find a comfortable, successful place in an integrated delivery system. In this chapter, I hope to share with you much of what I've learned so that you can find such a place for yourself.

The Basics

Let's start with the basics. To be successful in an integrated delivery system, it's important to understand what they are, why they're important, and at least something about how they're supposed to work.

What Is an Integrated Delivery System?

An integrated delivery system is a network of healthcare providers organized to deliver care to a defined population with certain health benefits. This sounds like gobbledygook, but it really boils down to a definition with two parts: care and money.

The *care* piece means that an integrated delivery system has a range and scope of services to meet the needs of the people being covered. Range and scope means that an integrated delivery system is geographically accessible and capable of handling the clinical needs of the "covered lives" (that's insurance-speak for people covered under an insurance plan). In order to handle diverse clinical needs, an integrated delivery system may include many types of professionals: counselor specialists, master's-trained therapists, Ph.D.s, and M.D.s. Integrated delivery systems also encompass many different treatment settings: outpatient offices, intensive outpatient programs, partial hospital programs, residential treatment, and inpatient programs.

The *money* piece refers to the fact that an integrated delivery system is accountable for the costs of care provided. The methods by which the integrated delivery system is held financially accountable vary considerably. It can be as specific as individual therapists being paid a set amount to provide all necessary care for each covered individual (termed *capitation*), or it can be as general as the threat of losing the contract if the integrated delivery system fails to meet the expectations of the contracting health plan. In either case, the viability of the integrated delivery system is inextricably linked to the financial dimension of the care it provides.

Integrated Delivery Systems Are Different from Independent Group Practices

An integrated delivery system isn't just structurally different from a less formal network; it also feels different. The financial risks and the system emphasis change how care is provided. Therapists in integrated delivery systems are often motivated to assess and stabilize patients twenty-four hours a day, rather than simply admitting them to the hospital and following up in the morning. Therapists tend to work more as a team and less with one discrete set of patients or clients. Treatment approaches are different, emphasizing outpatient and group therapies over inpatient and individual therapies. Professional roles tend to emphasize the unique capabilities of the professions—psychiatrists in psychopharmaceutical therapy, psychologists in testing—and utilize master's-trained staff more extensively in patient contact.

There are a few fundamental characteristics shared by all integrated delivery systems. There are many additional characteristics found in some integrated delivery systems. I've described some of the fundamental characteristics of integrated delivery systems in Table 6.1. If you are currently in an integrated delivery system, you may use this table to evaluate whether or not your system has met these fundamentals.

TABLE 6.1. FUNDAMENTAL CHARACTERISTICS OF AN INTEGRATED DELIVERY SYSTEM.

CHARACTERISTIC	DESCRIPTION
Capability to serve the needs of a diverse population	A range of services are available to care for differing needs of a covered population. Differing needs may include differing diagnoses, accessibility requirements, language considerations, or many other factors.
Diverse intensity of care	Care at different levels of intensity is available to facilitate the least intensive, yet clinically appropriate, level of care.
Established standards of care	The system establishes clinical, administrative, and service standards to which providers are expected to adhere.
Contracting capability	The system has some means to contract with employers, health plans, government programs, or other payers.
Administrative infrastructure	The system has the means to credential and decredential providers, manage finances, and monitor its business.
Governance structure	The system has a mission, an ownership, a governance process, and a management structure.

Why Are Integrated Delivery Systems Important?

Integrated delivery systems are important because managed care is important. The number of Americans covered by managed care has been growing steadily for the past twenty years. In 1973, there were fewer than 4 million Americans covered by HMOs. As of January 1, 1994, there were over 100 million Americans covered by various forms of managed behavioral healthcare plans. Experts forecast that this growth will continue for the foreseeable future.

Integrated delivery systems are the best way to provide care to people covered by managed care plans. This is not opinion; it is fact. The alternative to an integrated delivery system is a fragmented delivery system. An organized, integrated system is superior to a fragmented system *in providing managed care*. Whether managed care is good is an entirely different question and one I won't get into here; the assumption for purposes of this chapter is simply that managed care is important, so integrated delivery systems are important.

Examples of Integrated Delivery Systems

It may seem from the discussion above that all integrated delivery systems would be fairly similar to one another. Actually, they vary widely. They are all coordinated systems of behavioral healthcare providers designed to deliver care cost-effectively in a managed care environment, but the approaches used to reach this end are quite diverse. Consider the following examples of integrated delivery systems.

Henry Ford Health System. The Henry Ford Health System is one of the largest integrated delivery systems in the country. Operating multiple hospitals, the Henry Ford Medical Group, and its own HMO, it employs approximately one hundred mental health professionals. Psychiatrists, psychologists, and allied mental health professionals serve more than two hundred thousand people, predominantly through capitation arrangements. They have offices and locations throughout the Detroit metropolitan region. Included as part of the delivery system is a freestanding psychiatric hospital and a freestanding addictions treatment residential facility.

University Behavioral Group. University Behavioral Group is a network of psychiatrists and other mental health professionals serving the Houston metropolitan region. The group is owned by psychiatrists and has capitation and discounted fee-for-service contracts with health plans and directly with employers. The group has favorable financial arrangements with local psychiatric hospitals in order to permit appropriate and cost-effective hospitalization of patients.

Woodlands Treatment Center. Woodlands Treatment Center is a community mental health agency that has developed relationships with private managed care organizations. Located in Willmar, Minnesota, Woodlands Treatment Center serves a geographically dispersed rural area with a wide range of services and programs, including psychiatric, psychological, social work, education, partial hospitalization programs, a crisis unit, residential facilities, and intensive outpatient programs.

Shared Characteristics. All of these integrated delivery systems share the characteristics described in Table 6.1 but incorporate these features in very different ways. Table 6.2 illustrates the differences.

Other Differences Between Integrated Delivery Systems

While integrated delivery systems share certain fundamental characteristics, there are many different approaches to organization and operation.

TABLE 6.2. SHARED CHARACTERISTICS OF DIFFERENT INTEGRATED DELIVERY SYSTEMS.

	HENRY FORD HEALTH SYSTEM	UNIVERSITY BEHAVIORAL GROUP	WOODLANDS TREATMENT CENTER
Diverse populations	The largest mental health delivery system in the Detroit area.	Relatively small market share, but populations spread across Houston region.	Covering a large, rural geographic area.
Diverse intensity of care	Employs physicians, psychologists, and therapists. Owns hospital facilities.	Employs physicians and therapists, supplemented by a contracted network of physicians, therapists, and inpatient facilities.	A wide variety of services, including a limited number of psychiatrists, many therapists, several intensive ambulatory programs, and twenty-four-hour facilities.
Contracting	Provides services to managed care entities that are part of parent organization.	Vigorously competes for managed care and private employer contracts.	Preferred provider for dominant private insurer, as well as designated public provider.
Administrative infrastructure	Administered under aegis of parent organization.	Independent administrative structure.	Component of treatment center administration.
Governance	Owned by private parent corporation.	Owned by psychiatrists.	Public corporation sponsored by local governmental entities.

Provider Mix. Some integrated delivery systems rely heavily on master's-trained therapists, some rely more on clinical psychologists, and some on psychiatrists.

Treatment Philosophy. Some integrated delivery systems emphasize cost-effectiveness as their most important goal while others emphasize quality of service. Some adhere strictly to clinical guidelines while others provide clinical independence. Some use a medical model while others have a psychodynamic approach.

Integration with Other Health Care Services. Some integrated delivery systems are "behavioral healthcare carve-outs," meaning they are exclusively focused on behavioral healthcare and are not part of a larger health delivery system. Other integrated delivery systems cover all types of health care, not just behavioral health.

Geographical Focus. Some integrated delivery systems are local, some are regional, and some are national.

Ownership. Some integrated delivery systems are for-profit; others are not-for-profit. Some are owned by professional providers, some by hospitals, and some by investors. Investors owning behavioral integrated delivery systems include insurance companies, national managed care companies, pharmaceutical companies, and public shareholders directly.

Target Markets. Some integrated delivery systems target large multisite employers, some emphasize subcontracting behavioral services with HMOs, and others focus on Medicaid contracting.

Becoming Part of an Integrated Delivery System

Finding your place in an organized delivery system can mean either organizing a new integrated delivery system or participating in an already existing integrated delivery system. In this section, I talk about joining an existing integrated delivery system as well as the process of organizing a new one. In the next section, I show you how to be successful once you're in an integrated delivery system.

Joining an Existing Integrated Delivery System

There are several reasons why creating a new integrated delivery system may not be feasible or desirable. Your community may already be served by several very competitive integrated delivery systems. Or perhaps you have no interest in committing the time, energy, and expense required to create a new one. Or maybe there is already an integrated delivery system that you believe is compatible with your interests and abilities. In these cases, your best option may be to join an existing system.

There are three basic ways to become part of an existing integrated delivery system:

1. *Employment.* Becoming an employee is the simplest and most direct way for an individual to become part of an integrated delivery system. The hard part is often getting hired in the first place. The best advice in this regard is to know the right person. Most jobs are never advertised, but rather given to people the employer knows. If you don't know the right person at the system you want to work for, use people you do know to figure out who the right person is, and then develop a plan for getting that person to know you.

2. *Sale or Merger of Your Practice.* Many integrated delivery systems are interested in buying existing professional practices. This allows the system to acquire an organization, an existing patient base, and perhaps even existing payer relationships. The price to be paid will be negotiated considering a number of factors, including the number and motivation of potential buyers and the availability of alternative practices. The price should include two basic components: the cost of tangible assets, such as furniture and accounts receivable, and some intangible value which reflects your practice's status as an ongoing enterprise.

3. *Contracting.* The third possible way to join an existing integrated delivery system is to contract with it. This could mean covering a certain geographic area or providing a certain specialized service. The advantage of this approach is that it allows you to maintain your autonomy and perhaps at a later time pursue a different strategy. The disadvantage of this approach is that usually there is little security or long-term commitment associated with a contractual relationship.

Organizing a New Integrated Delivery System

Many people think organizing is as simple as performing tasks to accomplish a certain objective. The problem with this oversimplification is that it assumes the objective is known. But we know that integrated delivery systems take many different forms. So how do we know our objective, what we're trying to organize? In my opinion, organizing an integrated delivery system is 90 percent knowing the objective and only 10 percent doing the tasks which lead to the realization of the objective.

Setting your objective for an integrated delivery system requires an understanding of the following:

- The state of the art in behavioral healthcare
- The market you serve
- Your competition
- Your (and your organization's) own values, strengths, and weaknesses
- The opportunities available to you

If you don't examine these areas closely, your organizational efforts will be haphazard and poorly focused. You will lack a clear identity and will not be able to position yourself against competing systems.

Let's discuss these areas in more detail.

The State of the Art in Behavioral Healthcare. Behavioral healthcare standards of treatment are undergoing dramatic and radical change. Diagnostic and treatment approaches are often significantly different in a managed care environment than in many fee-for-service practices. The coverage of behavioral healthcare through health plans and the reimbursement for behavioral healthcare services have also been changing substantially. Here are some key national trends to be aware of:

- The dividing lines between public health and private health are dissolving. Increasingly, the same integrated delivery systems are serving both groups of people.
- A new dividing line is being drawn between "medically necessary" services that are covered by health plans and "elective" services, which must be paid out-of-pocket by the patient.
- Capitation and other forms of at-risk reimbursement are replacing traditional fee-for-service and discounted fee-for-service reimbursement.
- In a capitated environment the emphasis is on reducing costs, in contrast to a fee-for-service environment where the emphasis is on increasing revenue by finding patients.
- The mandate for cost-effectiveness is causing more emphasis on brief-therapy methods and outpatient or ambulatory treatment and less emphasis on long-term psychotherapy and inpatient treatment.
- Managing and demonstrating cost-effectiveness requires new systems for measuring and evaluating results.

Information about national trends is best obtained by attending conferences and keeping current with industry publications.

A common mistake is to try to organize an integrated delivery system for the purpose of protecting a particular treatment approach or philosophy. Free-standing psychiatric hospitals have often tried to develop integrated delivery systems for the purpose of increasing the use of their facilities. Psychiatrists and others have tried to preserve their practices by developing organizations to contract for managed care. These efforts are usually doomed. Meeting the market's expectations for state-of-the-art behavioral healthcare services is a requirement for success, even if it means closing hospital beds or abandoning a cherished treatment approach. Integrated delivery systems cannot sell treatment modalities that don't satisfy payer needs.

Meeting payers' needs doesn't mean that there's only one way of doing things. The destination of cost-effective care is predetermined, but the route you take to reach this destination is yours to choose. Integrated delivery systems across the country have shown that there are may ways to fulfill payer demands for cost-effectiveness, quality, and reasonable service.

Know Your Customers. Some behavioral healthcare professionals may not be accustomed to thinking of themselves as having customers. But behavioral health-care professionals wouldn't be reading this book if they weren't concerned about the success of their *business*. And business is all about serving the needs of customers.

The customers of a behavioral healthcare provider fall into three broad categories (the three P's): the public (or patients), the professional community (or providers), and payers. Each category has its own distinct needs:

- The public is generally interested in cost, convenience, and service. When covered by a health plan, costs may become a minor consideration because the individual often pays the same regardless of whom he or she sees. Managed care shifts the public's choice from choosing an individual professional at the time of need to choosing an integrated delivery system at the time of selecting a health plan.
- The professional community has more complex needs, reflecting its diverse nature. The professional community includes physicians, psychologists, social workers, counselors, clergy, school officials, and others. The needs of these professionals may include respecting professional boundaries, good communication, patient/client satisfaction, or potential for cross referral. Increasingly, professionals are having their referral choices restricted to affiliates within an integrated delivery system.
- Payers include insurance carriers, employers, government programs such as Medicare and Medicaid, HMOs, and PPOs. Enlightened payers are interested in maximizing the ratio between value of services provided and the cost of those services, while many other payers are interested in simply the lowest cost with a tolerable level of services. Meeting the needs of payers therefore requires both increasing the perception of value (by providing information about the quantity and quality of services rendered) and controlling the cost side of the equation.

Understanding customers in your market is more than knowing who they are. You also want to understand things like why they choose a certain therapist, how satisfied they are with the services available to them, and what changes they will be making.

There are many different ways to learn about your customers. Some of the more formal methods include focus groups, written or telephone surveys, and comment cards. A less formal approach is simply to talk to people. Also, there's often good information about healthcare customers published in local papers, collected by local associations, and available from your local hospital planning department.

Know Your Competition

There are basically two places your customers can get the services that you provide: from you or from your competitors. Thinking of the world this way, you'll realize that you really have many competitors even though there may not be any organization exactly like yours.

The best way to learn about competitors is to talk with colleagues, listen to your customers, and stay active in local professional organizations. Publications and conferences may also be important sources of information.

Know Yourself

It should come as no surprise to the therapist-reader that one of the most important elements of successfully organizing an integrated delivery system is having a good sense of your professional self. Some therapists feel quite comfortable with being part of an integrated delivery system that is committed to providing admittedly minimal care at the lowest possible cost. This philosophy may be justified because it makes some care accessible for many people who otherwise wouldn't get any. Other therapists are on the opposite end of the scale and don't believe they've fulfilled their ethical commitment until they've provided their patients with every possible treatment opportunity. Many therapists are in the middle, believing that good treatment opportunities should be available but recognizing that economics place some limits on the extent of these opportunities. It is unlikely that a therapist can be happy organizing or practicing in an integrated delivery system which has a business purpose in conflict with the therapist's own values.

In addition to your value system, it is important that you reflect upon and, to the extent possible, quantify your capabilities and resources. You may have organizational strengths and organizational weaknesses. There are probably services you can provide well and services you can't deliver. There are areas you understand and others you don't know well enough. You have finite resources to apply to the organizational effort.

Compare your capabilities and resources with the total capabilities and resources that will be needed to create the integrated delivery system. The difference between what you have and what you need is what you'll need to find elsewhere. A simple ledger sheet like that in Exhibit 6.1 may help you assess your capabilities and resources.

The Opportunity for Strategic Alliances

If you don't have all the capabilities or resources necessary to create an integrated delivery system, consider opportunities for strategic alliances. By forging a relationship with someone else, you may substantially increase the capabilities and

EXHIBIT 6.1. CAPABILITIES AND RESOURCES LEDGER.

	YOUR CAPABILITIES AND RESOURCES	TOTAL CAPABILITIES AND RESOURCES NEEDED	DIFFERENCE (WHAT YOU NEED FROM ANOTHER SOURCE)
Services available			
Geographic area covered			
Special population needs			
Organizational abilities			
Knowledge and expertise			
Time			
Money			

resources available to your organizational effort and, consequently, dramatically increase your likelihood of success.

One of the most important decisions to make is with whom the relationship will be. Perhaps it's natural to consider first a strategic partner who shares similar goals and philosophies. But you should also consider an individual or organization that is dissimilar, one that brings complementary resources and capabilities to the relationship. A therapist having a strategic alliance with, say, a hospital, as opposed to another therapist, has the advantage of each partner bringing to the relationship many things that the other partner does not have. A therapist brings clinical understanding and knowledge of the professional community, while the hospital brings money and organizational resources. On the other hand, dissimilar partners will have differing perspectives, goals, and philosophies, leading to challenges in creating good communications and trust. So weigh the pros and cons of potential alliances, but be aware that generally a similar partner makes internal relationship issues easier, while a dissimilar partner will make for a more complete set of resources and capabilities to compete in the external world. What do you need most in your particular situation?

The options available for strategic alliances are many and varied. If your organization is a professional practice, there may be good synergy with another professional practice that has a complementary geographic focus or mix of professional staff. Different types of behavioral healthcare organizations, such as hospitals, EAPs, or community mental health agencies, could add some otherwise inaccessible resources or relationships.

Ultimately, a strategic relationship must be based on a fundamental compatibility of respective goals and objectives. The process of creating the alliance should validate that such compatibility exists. Following the steps below helps ensure that the strategic alliance is based on a sound business relationship:

1. Define a shared strategic vision.
2. Define principles of a working relationship.
3. Explore opportunities for collaboration.
4. Prioritize opportunities.
5. Develop detailed business and operating plans.
6. Formalize the relationship.
7. Implement.

Niche or Be Niched

A key attribute of an effective strategy is that your integrated delivery system must occupy a unique niche. If there isn't something unique about your integrated delivery system, then there's no reason for customers to choose it. This unique aspect may be the composition of your provider network, or your geographic location; it could be your targeting special needs of certain populations; or it could be just about any difference or combination of differences that customers will recognize and value.

There are some niches that seem to attract integrated delivery systems like flies to flypaper. As the metaphor suggests, these niches often are a fatal attraction. One niche likely to fail is trying to distinguish your delivery system as the lowest-cost provider. This niche will attract customers with little loyalty, require unceasing dedication to finding new standards of low cost, and make you vulnerable to the new system with deep pockets that wants to buy market share. While low cost is normally a competitive element, there's an important difference between being cost competitive yet distinctive in other ways on the one hand, versus simply being the lowest-cost provider with no other apparent advantage.

Another fatal-attraction niche is being the high-quality system. High quality is an elusive attribute, certain to be challenged by other delivery systems which maintain they are of equally high quality but also have some other distinguishing advantages. High quality invites self-deception because it's hard to define and difficult to quantify. To be a truly competitive attribute, quality should be defined in the customer's terms rather than your own. Like low cost, quality is important to have; but it is not usually an effective way of defining a niche.

An effective process for identifying a niche involves comparing and contrasting the attributes of your delivery system with the needs of your target customers, and with the capabilities of your competitors. Evaluate your current practice, considering both why your customers choose you and the major elements of your philosophy. Now consider the customers you hope to reach through your integrated delivery system: what do they want and need? How have they been making choices? Finally, evaluate your competitors and the way they distinguish themselves, both positively and negatively. Your niche is a place that fits with what you are and satisfies your customers better than the alternatives do.

Organize and Implement

Now that you know your destination, it's time to plan the trip that will take you there. Your "itinerary" has these components:

- A statement of values, or mission statement, which is the moral compass by which your organization will be guided
- A strategic plan, which sets out the assumptions about your market, your customers, your competitors, and yourself, describing why your delivery system will be successful in a competitive environment
- An operating plan, probably the most detailed and complex element of your plans, outlining the capabilities your delivery system will have, how they will be organized, and how they will evolve from inception through full operation
- A marketing plan, identifying your target customers, describing how you will reach them with your message, and specifying the price, product, place, and promotions you'll be offering
- An action plan, listing who is going to do what by when in order to implement your operational and marketing plans
- A financial plan, projecting the money needed to subsidize starting up and reaching profitable operations, identifying where the money will come from, and estimating what return can be expected

Once the above plans have been created, reconciled with each other, rendered doable, and based on reasonable assumptions, you're ready for the fun part: implementation.

Pitfalls to Avoid

Experience has shown there are several common mistakes leading to the failure of efforts to develop an integrated delivery system. In the hope that you may avoid them, they are

- Failure to act. There are far more opportunities than are ever realized. Realizing rewards requires taking risk. Be decisive and persevering. Ready, fire! Then *aim*, and fire again.
- Trying to do too much. Be realistic about your resources and capabilities. Consider sharing your burden; it's better to own a percentage of a success than to own all of a failure.
- Form before function. Healthcare is rife with fads. If you think you have the answer, but you're not sure of the question, proceed with caution.
- Confusing what you want with what the customer wants. There's no surer road to disappointment than trying to implement a strategy that involves repackaging what the market has already said it doesn't want.

Succeeding in an Integrated Delivery System

Now that you're in an integrated delivery system, how are you going to find success, happiness, and prosperity? Many professionals who work in integrated delivery systems enjoy being able to focus on their area of expertise and not worry about extraneous aspects of healthcare delivery. They appreciate the camaraderie and collegiality of being part of a larger organization, having professional and support resources to draw upon, and benefiting from the security of being part of a relatively predictable business. On the other hand, many other people in integrated delivery systems complain about bureaucracy, unreasonable workloads, restrictions, rules, meetings, administrators, and other hassles.

How can you enjoy the benefits and minimize the drawbacks of working in an integrated delivery system? The key is to understand the objectives of the system and determine how to align your personal objectives with those of the system. Let's explore the system's objectives and then discuss finding a comfortable role for you.

Goals of an Integrated Delivery System

Different integrated delivery systems have different missions and values. However, there are basic operational capabilities that every integrated delivery system strives for. Understanding how your particular delivery system plans to realize these capabilities is a starting point for realizing happiness and success in the organization. These fundamental capabilities include

- *Aligning the interests of caregivers with the interests of the delivery system.* The delivery system must have physicians, therapists, and facilities providing care in a manner consistent with the business objectives of the system. Employing or owning caregiving resources, imposing rules and restrictions, and sharing economic risk are common approaches to getting the caregivers to behave in a manner consistent with what the delivery system is trying to accomplish.
- *Serving the diverse needs of customers.* Integrated delivery systems are responsible for providing care to a diverse range of people with many different needs. Fulfilling these needs cost-effectively is a major challenge and a central purpose of integrated delivery systems.
- *Improving the cost-effectiveness of care.* The standards of cost-effective care are continuing to evolve. Alternatives to hospitalization are continuing to drive down inpatient utilization, while new outpatient programs and group therapy approaches continue to be developed. Integrated delivery systems want the cost of care to decline, preferably without diminishing quality or accessibility.
- *Coordinating care.* Integrated delivery systems want patients to be able to access care in a straightforward fashion and be referred to the appropriate therapist and intensity of treatment as their changing situation warrants. This usually requires a central access point for people to call. It also requires good coordination and communications between different components of the delivery system.
- *User friendliness.* As patients receive care through what is supposed to be a single delivery system, they may feel frustrated and confused if they are expected to complete new paperwork when they're seen at different locations, undergo multiple assessments, repeat histories, call different phone numbers, and learn different routines. Integrated delivery systems are interested in eliminating these inconveniences and appearing to consumers as a single comprehensive entity whose "right hand knows what the left hand is doing."
- *Marketability.* Integrated delivery systems want existing and prospective customers to have a positive impression of their services. Accomplishing this requires satisfying customers, projecting a positive image, developing a reputation for service, and actively communicating positive information.

Healthy Versus Dysfunctional Integrated Delivery Systems

Most integrated delivery systems pursue their business objectives in a rational fashion. Although it may not appear this way to everyone in the organization, decision processes consider the available choices, evaluate the relative merits of different options, and lead to implementation of the chosen policy. Managers manage, operations operate, and the delivery system delivers.

Of course, even rational integrated delivery systems enjoy varying degrees of success in accomplishing their objectives. Differing circumstances, missions, management capabilities, available resources, and other factors have a substantial impact on the relative success of any given integrated delivery system. Most organizations don't completely succeed in accomplishing their missions. Most people who work within an integrated delivery system are part of an organization that is trying to be successful and having incomplete success in doing so. Regardless, it is possible for most people in these integrated delivery systems to be fulfilled and feel professionally satisfied.

There are two situations where an individual will be unable to attain personal satisfaction working in an integrated delivery system. The first is when the integrated delivery system is dysfunctional. Just like people, in any industry there are some organizations unable to function in a healthy, rational fashion. The second untenable situation is when your individual values are not reconcilable with the values of your delivery system. If either situation exists, your options are to leave the organization, try to change your values or the organization's, or endure.

Finding Your Place in the Integrated Delivery System

Once you see what the system is trying to accomplish, a place for you in the system can be found by aligning your role with the system's goals. There are many roles to play in an integrated delivery system, including direct provision of care, development of the clinical delivery system, management of care delivery, administration, and marketing.

Finding your place requires defining your role and performing your role. In taking each of these steps, consider both your own needs and the organization's needs. When you discover roles for you to play which harmonize your interests, abilities, and talents with meeting the organization's needs, you will be well on your way to professional happiness and success. I wish you the very best!

CHAPTER SEVEN

MANAGED CARE CONTRACTING

Helen A. White

Clinicians in practice and administrators of facilities and programs build their businesses through contracting with a variety of sources: managed care entities, employers, employer coalitions, insurance companies, healthcare systems, and federal as well as state agencies (Medicaid, Medicare, CHAMPUS).

Contracting with a Managed Care Organization (MCO)

Providers are becoming more aware of the financial need to contract with as many managed care organizations as possible in order to increase or maintain their patient base. Typically, the first step in establishing a relationship with an MCO is entering into a contract. This chapter explains the steps of the contracting process, how to achieve the greatest impact in "selling" your services through the contracting and application process with an MCO, and how to avoid pitfalls in the contracting process.

The Advantages of Contracting with an MCO

The advantages of contracting with an MCO amount to more than the financial incentive of increasing patient volume. Contracting with MCOs also provides you with the opportunity to

- Identify your business costs, as well as therapy, evaluations, and administrative costs. Avoid or minimize risk by more carefully examining your current business practices.
- Modify or change your business practices to adjust to changes in reimbursement methodology and payment incentive.
- Learn more about your patients' insurance plans and their covered benefits. Specifically, review the differences in benefits offered among the different MCOs, as well as what percentage of your practice is tied to these MCOs.
- Know the employers in your area; they are another source of referrals. Which insurance plans do they use? When do they make decisions to review contracts and consider new plans? Can you provide services to any of their employees through their current contract arrangements? Learn which employers are considering electing an MCO to manage their employees' health benefits. Can you position yourself with the employer before they sign a contract? If your patients' employers change insurance plans and benefits, your practice may change as well.
- Examine your clinical practice profile:
  Types and ages of patients you are treating
  Your hours of operation
  Ease of access, for convenience of patients or for a "service orientation"
  Your special skills, interests, and experiences
  The status of your credentials and continuing education efforts

What You Need to Know About the MCO

There are hundreds of MCOs in existence. Some are currently accepting providers into their networks, while others have closed their panels. Whether you are under contract or in the process of contracting with an MCO, there are several questions you should ask about its operations.

What Is the MCO's Administrative Structure? Inquire about the MCO's medical director—who she is and how she fits into the organizational chain of command. What experience do the top managers have in managed care operations, finance, claims payment, provider relations, and member services? This information gives you an understanding of the probable success of the MCO.

What Is the Financial Status of the MCO and Its Record of Performance? Inquire about the founders, financial backers, and operators of the MCO. (You can obtain this information from your state insurance department, Dun and Bradstreet, or the MCO itself.) If you are dealing with a newly formed MCO, examine its financial performance. As with most new businesses, the first two years are critical and the MCO may lose money. This does not necessarily mean that you should contract only with well-established MCOs; there is a history of long-lived MCOs filing bankruptcy. The object of your research is to determine if the MCO is financially solvent and has the financial resources to support its business.

Can the MCO Perform Its Responsibilities? The MCO's responsibilities include providing referrals, hiring and training a clinical staff to discuss and certify benefits treatment plans, clarifying policies and procedures, and managing and paying claims in a timely manner. Does the MCO have the administrative staff, organizational structure, and financial resources to meet its contractual obligations to clinicians, facilities, programs, employers, etc?

What Is the MCO's Payment Structure? Does the MCO application include the MCO's proposed payment structure? Does the fee structure provide sufficient information on services, treatments, and programs covered?

What Policies and Procedures Should the MCO Have in Place? At a minimum, the MCO should have written policies and procedures for grievances and an appeals process; utilization review; selection and credentialing criteria; claims filing and payments; and so forth.

How Does the MCO Manage Issues of Patient Confidentiality? How is patient information provided to the MCO to maintain confidentiality? How and where are the patients' files and records maintained? Is the MCO required to inform other professionals or entities of the patient's access to behavioral healthcare benefits? Does the patient sign a release form before the information is provided to others?

The Contracting Process

After evaluating an MCO and making the decision to pursue a relationship, the next step is the contracting process. There are two major steps: completing the application and executing the contract or agreement. It is strongly suggested that you review the contract before completing the application. It takes an average of two to five hours to complete an application and obtain copies of required ancillary documents. If the contract raises concerns or may negatively impact your business, then you do not want to spend valuable time and resources completing the application and collecting supporting documents until your concerns are resolved.

Most of the contracts used by MCOs today are considered boilerplate, that is, they include standard sections in legal language. However, each MCO contract may vary significantly when it comes to provider responsibilities, claim filing procedures and payments, or penalties that may be assessed for failure to abide by the rules.

Specific Contract Sections for Careful Review

In studying the entire MCO provider contract, be aware that some sections require a more thorough understanding than others. The most significant sections are those having an impact on the financial structure and projections of your business (provider reimbursement and factors that affect provider payment) and those impacting clinical aspects of your business (provider responsibilities).

Provider Reimbursement. To many providers the most important page of the contract is the one that deals with the method and amount of reimbursement. There are various types of reimbursement: discounted fee schedules, capitation, discount arrangements, per diem, and program and case rates. Although the payment methodology is always part of the contract, not all MCO contracts specify the actual fees to be paid in the contract. For example, one Fortune 500 MCO lists only one current procedural terminology (CPT) code with related fee in its contract; another national MCO's contract does not include any fee information.

If you receive a contract that does not specify the fees you will receive for providing services, call the MCO and ask for a fee schedule. It is the policy of some companies not to send fee schedules, but they should give you the information over the phone. Make a list of your most frequently billed CPT codes, noting your fees for the services next to the codes. List the MCO's reimbursement fees next to yours for comparison.

Negotiating fee schedules or rates is usually possible for facilities and programs, occasionally for multidisciplinary groups, but seldom for individual clinicians. Negotiating fee schedules with clinicians is usually limited to those who provide an expertise or skill that is not readily available from other clinicians within a specific geographical location. At best the MCO may negotiate one or two specific CPT codes for that clinician or group.

Facilities and programs are often sent blank rate sheets with their contracts. The MCO expects the facility to complete and return the rate sheet with its best prices for services or else to call the facility to negotiate the rates. This step initiates the rate negotiation process between the MCO and facility and/or program. You need to know your average per diem costs, rates of negotiated contracts, average regional per diem rates, amount of expected business, the potential value of this contract, and your current patient mix by payer type. In general, facilities list their expected rates, and in turn the MCO either negotiates or accepts the rates.

When reviewing the reimbursement schedule, check to see if the payments cover all the products offered by the MCO or if they vary for different products. MCOs do vary reimbursement significantly by product or line of business, examples being commercial, Medicaid, Medicare, or seniors plans, and CHAMPUS (for retired military and their dependents).

There are various types of provider reimbursement. The following section describes these methods and explains some of the terms associated with provider reimbursement, including definitions, descriptions, and other related information.

Fee Schedule. A fee schedule consists of a list of professional fees associated with the most common services or CPT codes used by a specific group of providers, such as psychiatrists, psychologists, social workers, and counselors. In the behavioral healthcare arena there often is a separate fee schedule for each discipline, linked to CPT codes. Compare the MCO's fee schedule with other contracts and against your established charges to determine if there are significant differences in reimbursement and if the reimbursement rates are acceptable.

The ability to negotiate professional fees depends on several factors:

• The MCO's market share or penetration in your area
• Your practice location and the specialty you offer
• The support of other professionals in negotiating changes
• The average fees of other managed care firms in your area

In general, it is rare or impossible for an individual clinician to negotiate increases in the fee schedule with a major behavioral healthcare MCO. But there is some chance for a group of clinicians to negotiate an increase if they are strategically positioned in their region.

For example: A mental health MCO was recently awarded a contract from an HMO to provide behavioral healthcare services to ninety thousand members in the western region of a large state. The MCO was a relatively young organization and new to the region. Initial efforts to recruit board-certified psychiatrists failed completely because the area psychiatrists all stated that the fee payments for evaluation and medication management were too low. They declined to join the network. The MCO needed board certified psychiatrists and therefore decided to increase the fees. Each psychiatrist was personally notified by telephone and sent a letter in which they were informed of the increase in professional fees for the specified services.

Another example: A multidisciplinary group practice located in one of the

Mid-Atlantic states was considered "very managed care unfriendly." The MCO needed these clinicians to provide services to its members. The group was not able to negotiate an across-the-board increase in the fee schedule; but it was able to secure an agreement to receive a significant portion of the MCO's referrals.

Capitation Rates. Capitation is a fixed payment amount per month for each member in a specific geographical area. The term frequently used to describe capitation payment is PMPM, or per member per month. The payment rate is derived by analyzing the utilization of services (actual and target), the average cost of services, and the demographics of the number of covered lives.

For behavioral healthcare clinicians, contracts for capitation reimbursement are usually limited to multidisciplinary group practices. In a capitated arrangement, the practice is required to pay for the services rendered by its professionals as well as any nongroup behavioral healthcare professionals who may be needed to provide services to the member population. If the group expects to refer to professionals outside its practice, it would be wise to negotiate fees prior to any referrals for treatment since the fees will be deducted from the PMPM revenue.

The term *risk pool* refers to the part of the capitation payment that is withheld by the MCO from the practice to cover greater than expected expenses for hospitalization, out-of-area referrals, or catastrophic cases. The contract will describe how and when the risk pool payment is made, expected utilization targets, as well as any amount of money that may be withheld. The contract must specify the exact method of determining the risk pool and when the funds are returned to the practice. In addition, the contract language usually specifies how surpluses are calculated and when they are distributed to the practice. This type of risk arrangement should be examined carefully for its feasibility and suitability to the provider group. The language should also specify deficit calculations and repayments to the MCO by the practice.

For example, suppose the capitation payment is calculated at $2 PMPM for fifteen thousand members within specific zip codes. The monthly capitation payment would be $30,000. The MCO holds 20 percent of the monthly capitation payment in a "risk pool." The MCO and practice periodically reconcile the services provided to the members against the targeted utilization. If the practice meets the targeted utilization rates, it receives the money that was held in the risk pool, which is termed a "bonus." If the practice exceeds the targeted utilization rates and maintains quality and delivery of care, it shares in the MCO's savings. If the practice is not able to meet the targeted utilization, it will be penalized—not only forfeiting the "bonus" but possibly required to pay back prepaid fees for exceeding the targeted utilization rates.

MCOs contracting under capitation reimbursement generally establish a floor or ceiling for utilization rates. The MCO sets parameters in an attempt to ensure the quality of care delivered by the provider, while it protects the provider against unexpected catastrophic cases.

Capitation rates are no longer limited to clinicians or group practices. MCOs are also approaching facility administrators to consider capitation rates for inpatient and outpatient services. To avoid a negative impact on their business and services, facilities entering into a capitated reimbursement method must clearly understand the cost of delivering services.

Discounted Fees. Discounted fees are just that: fees typically discounted 25–45 percent in exchange for the MCO referrals. If the MCO offers a discount fee arrangement, the provider needs to know if the discount is taken from the provider's charges or from the standardized charges, also known as "usual, customary, and reasonable," or UCR. The UCR charges are established by the MCO for specific geographical areas. MCOs typically offer discounted fee structures to both clinicians and facility providers.

In connection with discounted fee payments, "withhold" is a mechanism by which the MCO retains a portion of the fee-for-service provider's payments against overutilization of services. It is similar to the capitation risk pool. The difference between the withhold and risk-pool arrangements is when, or in what proportion, payment will be paid to the provider. Withholds are usually paid to providers at the end of the year. If there are no extra medical expenses, the entire withhold is returned to the providers. If some of the money was paid to cover the extra expenses, a reduced portion of the withhold is returned. How and to whom the portion of the money is paid is based on profiles of providers' utilization patterns developed by the MCO. Those providers who manage the care of the MCO's members in the most cost-effective manner will receive a portion of the withhold in return. The provider who consistently exceeds the estimated costs of care will not be reimbursed a portion of the withhold. This is the MCO's attempt to distribute the funds more equitably and offer incentives to providers to manage care in the most cost-effective manner.

Intensive Case Management Rate. The intensive case management rate is a negotiated fixed rate for services provided to a specific patient that includes intensive professional services as an alternative to inpatient placement. The cases selected for intensive case management are usually patients who have not responded successfully to previous treatment encounters. By mutual agreement the clinician and MCO believe the needs of the patient would best be served by providing intensive professional services in a limited time frame with a defined outcome. The clinician determines how often she will meet with the patient in order to achieve the goals. For example, appointments might be twice a day, several times a week, for four weeks in duration. Interim reports are made to the MCO's case manager to discuss the patient's progress and whether treatment goals remain reasonable and achievable. For these services, the clinician is paid a negotiated case or flat rate for her services.

Per Diem Rates. A per diem rate is a fixed payment for services provided each day to a patient receiving care in an inpatient facility or outpatient program. The per diem rate for an inpatient day or outpatient program day includes all services: nursing, ancillary, lab, radiology, pharmacy, psychological testing, counseling, etc. In many regions of the country, MCOs are negotiating the inclusion of attending physician services within per diem rates. Different per diem rates are usually established for intensity and type of services, such as detoxification, acute inpatient, intensive structured-type outpatient programs, partial hospital programs, as well as services for adults, adolescents, or children.

The ranges for the per diem rates that the MCO is willing to negotiate with a facility are usually based on regional differences, cost of living, average incomes, and other market forces. In order to negotiate a per diem rate, you need to know your minimum acceptable per diem rate, the value of the contract to your business (how many referrals you may receive), your value to the MCO, and whether your competition has a contract with the MCO. If the competition has negotiated rates and contracted with the MCO, the MCO may decide it does not need your services unless your proposed rates are equal to or lower than those of your competitor offering similar services.

Per Diem Rates with Maximum Program Rate. Per diem rates with a maximum program rate establish a fixed price for the length of the treatment program. For example, an intensive structured outpatient program (ISOP) is designed to provide a broad range of activities and therapy services for four to eight weeks, with an additional six to twelve months of aftercare. The fees negotiated for this program might be a per diem rate of $65 with a program maximum of $2,000. This financial incentive encourages the program to carefully monitor patient treatment and achieve optimum outcomes in the time frame covered. MCOs are now negotiating a reduced program rate in case of relapse or readmission of the same patient within a specified period of time. This serves to build in added confidence that quality of care and optimal treatment will be carefully monitored by the provider.

Percent of Charges. Percent of charges is a reimbursement method by which a discount off a facility's published charges is negotiated. The discount can range from 5 to 50 percent. The facility is required to submit its published charges prior to the negotiation. This form of payment is not favored by a majority of the managed care companies because facilities raise their charges annually. Therefore, the costs for care continue to spiral upward.

Case Rates. A case rate is an all-inclusive rate paid for both inpatient and professional services for a specific procedure or diagnosis. Examples of the types of medical procedures for which case rates are negotiated are obstetrical care, coronary artery bypass surgery, and bone marrow transplant. Behavioral healthcare MCOs are also contracting with providers for case rates for the treatment of selected mental health or substance abuse disorders.

For example, a patient with a substance abuse problem requires detoxification and follow-up treatment. Under the case rate agreement, the provider agrees to render all appropriate services to the member, including detox, inpatient, outpatient, and aftercare services, for one all-inclusive fee. If the patient relapses, the provider is obligated to continue treatment for the length of the contract arrangements without additional payments.

Bed Leasing. Although not a common practice, some facilities have contracted with MCOs to lease a specific number of beds in exchange for a flat monthly rate. The payment is made to the facility whether the beds are occupied or not. A question faced with this reimbursement model is whether the MCO realizes any real savings based on current reductions in inpatient utilization.

Periodic Interim Payments or Cash Advances. Periodic interim payments or cash advance contracts with behavioral healthcare facilities are paid by an agency or MCO for future services expected to be rendered to members. A reconciliation between the two parties is conducted at least annually. This type of reimbursement provides the facility with positive cash flow. The facility must have the capability and experience to evaluate and monitor the cost of care, manage the cost based on the cycles of the delivery of care, and have the cash reserves to either return the surplus to the paying agency or meet the deficits incurred.

For example, a large Midwest healthcare system provides the majority of services for the city's Medicaid population and receives quarterly payments from the state for the services. Four years ago, the health system began experiencing a downward spiral in financial stability due to loss of several managed care contracts, poor investment strategies, and settlements of several lawsuits. To meet its financial obligations, the health system began using the periodic interim payments to meet its day-to-day operational needs. Consequently, the financial situations of both the health system and the paying agency fell into jeopardy and both went into bankruptcy.

Payer Reinsurance. Reinsurance, purchased by the MCO, is a financial safeguard for the providers. If the MCO cannot meet its financial obligations and becomes insolvent, then reinsurance

- Allows a continuation of benefits to members for the time their premiums were collected
- Provides coverage for hospitalized members
- Allows conversion to individual policies without evidence of insurability

Reinsurance is an important contract provision for you because it guarantees payment of claims if the MCO does not meet its financial responsibilities due to insolvency.

If the reinsurance section is missing, request that the MCO insert a clause in your contract stating it has payer insurance, and ask for a copy of the reinsurance face sheet.

Stop-Loss Insurance. Stop-loss insurance, sometimes referred to as catastrophic insurance, usually covers medical expenses that exceed a certain dollar amount per patient. This insurance option guarantees that the full risk of unexpectedly high utilization of services is not passed on to the provider. In a discounted fee-for-services model, the stop-loss insurance is provided for the contracted professional services only. In the capitation model, the stop-loss insurance is applied to a specific case, that is, one that exceeds the predetermined costs for care.

For example, in the discounted fee-for-service model 20 percent of the annual inpatient expenses are projected at $7,000 for the attending physician's fees. Because of trauma and unexpected circumstances, five patients of a psychiatrist's practice require extensive inpatient treatment, thus exceeding the projected costs. The stop-loss insurance covers the expenses in excess of the $7,000.

A sample case in the capitation model might be a group practice paid $3 PMPM for managing acute mental health inpatient care with a targeted length of stay of nine days. One dollar PMPM is withheld in a risk pool. Due to treatment complications and discharge placement difficulties, an adolescent patient of the group practice remains in the hospital for eighteen days. The stop-loss insurance is applied to the specific case.

"Favored Nations" Clause. The "favored nations" clause is designed to protect an MCO from its competition by ensuring that providers who contract with it cannot offer a lower rate to any other MCO. The favored-nations clause states that if a provider offers a new, lower rate to another MCO, then that discount must also be extended to the first MCO regardless of the negotiated amount previously contracted. This clause appears frequently in facility contracts and is becoming more common in group provider agreements.

For example: The vice president of operations (VPO) at a 350-bed facility secures a contract with a national MCO that has a contract with the largest employer in the facility's area. As part of the negotiation, the facility agreed to a per diem rate that was lower than any of its other contracts. The VPO's rationale for the rate was access to a significant portion of new business. The facility also had a contract with Blue Cross Blue Shield. The VPO was unaware of the Blue Cross Blue Shield favored-nations contract requirements. When the VPO informs his senior executive team of the new contract and rate, the vice president of finance says the Blue Cross Blue Shield contract represents 46 percent of the facility's inpatient business, and that it has a favored-nations clause. The facility is now required to apply the same discounted rate it negotiated with the new MCO to its Blue Cross Blue Shield contract.

Provider Responsibilities

Provider responsibilities are described in a variety of sections in an MCO contract. Although section titles vary among contracts, the following are usually included in all contracts:

> Definition of terms
>
> Filing of claims
>
> Billing patients for services
>
> Compliance with utilization review standards and quality assurance program
>
> Provider services
>
> Nondiscrimination of services
>
> Maintenance of records
>
> Confidentiality and reporting requirements
>
> Grievance procedures

Each contract usually presents the definition of terms used by the MCO in the provider contract. Compare the definitions of the terms with their use in the body of the contract to ensure consistency between the definition and its interpretation when used in the text. It is also important to review the provider manual, particularly if the contract makes reference to adherence to the rules in the manual.

Filing Claims. The contract should state how, when, and where to file a claim. In order to file a claim you may be required to submit the claim on a standard HCFA 1500 or similar form. If you use a form other than HCFA 1500, verify its acceptability with the MCO. If you have the capability of electronic transfer of claims, ask the MCO if it permits electronic filing for claims. This section may also state when you must file a claim after providing services.

For example, you may file a claim after your initial evaluation of the patient, weekly, or every thirty days, regardless of whether or not the patient has been discharged from treatment. If the expected length of time for reimbursement for a submitted claim is not stated in the body of the contract, ask the MCO. Also ask how often the MCO meets its time goals in reimbursing claims. Some MCOs require claims to be submitted within a certain number of days of providing service, or at the end of the fiscal year, particularly if withhold or risk arrangements are in place.

The contract usually refers to the provider manual for details related to completing and filing a claim. Although the provider manual is part of the contracting process, many MCOs will not distribute the manual prior to contract unless specifically asked by the provider. The provider manual is usually included with facility contracts. It is important to recognize that MCOs will not make changes to their provider manuals, because they are the operations manuals for MCOs.

Patient Billing. MCO contracts specifically state the situations in which providers can bill or collect fees from a member. Generally there are only two instances when a provider can bill or collect fees directly from a member:

1. When the member is required to pay a copayment amount
2. When there has been a denial of benefits and the member requests the clinician to provide the services regardless of the denial

Usually the provider must secure from the member, in writing and prior to treatment, agreement to accept financial responsibility for the services provided. The MCO may require that the provider use the MCO's form for this purpose.

Other than the situations described above, providers are usually prohibited from billing the member, regardless of such conditions as short notice cancellations of appointments, no-shows for scheduled appointments, or even bankruptcy of the MCO. In the event of a pattern of cancellations or no-shows by a member, the provider can notify the MCO (usually through the MCO's provider relations department) of the problem. If an MCO does have a policy that allows the provider to bill the patient for no-shows, the policy for billing the patient must be in writing. The member is usually required to sign a statement of the billing policy related to no-shows, prior to treatment. If the problem is not resolved within a reasonable period of time, the provider can request removal of the patient from her practice.

Compliance with Utilization Review and Quality Assurance Programs. This section of the contract states that the provider is obligated to comply with the MCO's utilization review standards and quality assurance programs. The details of standards and programs are located in the provider manual. As a clinician contracting with an MCO for the first time, you need to obtain from the MCO your specific responsibilities regarding utilization review and quality assurance program.

Provider Services/Performance Requirements. The services to be performed by the provider are specified either in the body of the contract or in an exhibit. You need to know to whom you are obligated to provide services, how member eligibility is determined, and who is assigned the responsibility for payment if the services are furnished to a noncovered person. You also need to review the contract requirements regarding referring to other providers and accepting referrals from other clinicians; your expected response time for the cases of emergency, urgent, and routine referrals, etc.

Carefully evaluate your ability to meet performance requirements. For example, one of the national behavioral healthcare MCOs requires the provider to respond to referrals within these time frames: respond to emergency call within thirty minutes by phone and see the patient within two hours; respond to urgent calls within thirty minutes by phone and see the patient within twenty-four hours; and make appointments for routine referrals within three days.

Nondiscrimination of Services. This language in the contract typically states that the provider will provide services to members in the same manner that he provides to nonmanaged care members or other commercial members. It means you cannot treat a patient differently because of the source of payment or because he or she is a Medicaid beneficiary. Discriminatory practices include setting preferred office hours, specific days, or establishing waiting times for specific patient groups. This clause also prohibits any discrimination on the basis of race, color, sex, religion, disability, and national origin under federal, state, and local law.

Maintenance of Records, Confidentiality, and Reporting Requirements

The contract usually states your responsibilities related to maintaining files in accordance with federal and state laws, providing copies of the files to the MCO within a stated time frame, etc. It is helpful to know your administrative costs, such as time and expenses for maintaining files, copying records, and sending them to the MCO; and the time required to meet the reporting requirements. Inquire if there is reimbursement by the MCO for any of these expenses. Some MCOs, in accordance with state regulations, will pay facility providers a flat fee, for example $25, for copying a patient's record.

Grievance Procedures. A grievance may be filed by a provider for a variety of issues: utilization management, payment errors, disagreements with peer review decisions, denial of benefits, etc. The details of the grievance process are in the provider manual. The contract states what mechanism exists for filing a grievance and the method of dispute resolution, such as mediation, arbitration, or litigation.

An example of a situation in which a provider might file a grievance is if the benefit plan includes twenty annual visits for psychotherapy but the case manager authorizes six visits and then denies further benefits because of a difference of opinion regarding treatment plan. Another example is failure to pay claims, or consistent delays in payment or payment errors. The MCO may also file a grievance against a provider for performance deficiencies.

Credentialing Requirements. The contract will state the requirement for the provider to maintain current professional liability insurance in amounts defined by either the MCO or state regulations. In addition, the contract will state that the provider is expected to meet and maintain her credentialing requirements for participation in the network. The details of the credentialing requirements are located in the provider manual and usually include type of license, minimum experience requirements, certifications, current Drug Enforcement Agency (DEA) certificate (for M.D. or D.O. only), current curriculum vitae, and so forth.

Other Contract Clauses

Hold Harmless Clause. The "hold harmless" clause indicates that one of the contracted parties is relieved of any liability related to the treatment of an MCO member. If the clause is in the contract, it can shift the contractual liability to the provider if the MCO is sued in connection with treatment ordered by the provider for a member. Therefore, it is suggested that you *not* sign the contract, or at least amend the language to state that each party is solely responsible for their actions and neither can be held liable for the actions of the other.

The MCO is established to manage, authorize, or deny benefits, not to render care or treatment. They are making a benefit determination. Review the contract for language that requires you, the provider, to inform the member of the right to appeal the decision to the MCO when care or treatment is denied.

For example, you inform your patient you cannot treat him with a specific therapeutic intervention, which later results in a relapse or readmission to the hospital and loss of his job. Your patient files a suit against the MCO and you. You become liable because you did not tell the patient that he can appeal that decision to the MCO. Such a clause or wording indemnifies the MCO (holds it harmless) for the results of your actions.

Notifications. The contract usually describes the process of how a provider is notified of changes in policies, provider services, fees, products, and so forth. The notification clause also describes the process the MCO must follow if an event such as loss of license, bankruptcy, or felony materially impairs the MCO's ability to perform its duties under the contract. Conversely, the clause requires the providers to inform the MCO of any changes in their operations that materially impair their ability to provide services (malpractice awards, bankruptcy, embezzlement) or any actions taken against it by licensing, federal, and state regulatory bodies and private accrediting agencies.

For example, a facility contracted with an MCO to provide inpatient services for children, adolescents, and adults. The facility was investigated and found guilty by the state of fraudulently billing for Medicare and Medicaid services. As a result, the facility lost its license to treat the Medicare and Medicaid population. The facility is required to notify the MCO of the impending investigation as well as the results of the investigation.

Cancellation and Termination Clauses. The contract cancellation and termination clauses describe situations by which the MCO can immediately terminate its contract with a provider, e.g., loss of license, unresolved and repeated member complaints, failure to meet provider contract responsibilities, etc. Either party, the MCO or the provider, can cancel the contract with written notification to the other party. The contract typically requires a minimum time for the effective date of the cancellation, such as sixty or ninety days.

◆ ◆ ◆

Clinicians and administrators have and will continue to have successful contractual relationships with MCOs. The contracting process is not and should not be an adversarial relationship. To be successful, it should be considered mutually beneficial to both parties—provided each party understands, agrees to, and meets the obligations of the contract.

A clinician should consult an experienced healthcare lawyer when a section or several sections of the contract are unclear or indicate some risk and are not resolved in discussions with the MCO. To find a lawyer with healthcare-contract experience, call your local chapter of the American Bar Association, your professional association, local hospitals, and so forth. Facilities often have their contracts reviewed by their legal counsel to be assured that the facility's operational capability meets its contractual responsibilities. Once facilities and programs become familiar with the contracting process and standard language, they usually minimize the use of legal counsel for contract review.

The success of contracting is based on a clear understanding of several factors:

- Your business: your goals, capabilities, administrative costs, financial requirements, patient panel targets, and so forth
- Managed care processes: utilization review, quality assurance programs, reporting requirements, reimbursement processes, and so forth
- The potential value of contracting with the MCO: patient referrals, improving your financial projections, and so forth
- The contract requirements, specifically the contractual obligations of the provider and the MCO

The Application

MCOs typically require providers to submit an application for consideration as a network provider. The application is an opportunity for you to demonstrate to the MCO the potential value of your services. You are usually required to list the demographics of your practice; your services; your professional or staff skills, expertise, and experience; accreditation and licenses; and other pertinent information.

How you package yourself can make a tremendous difference. A "winning" application meets the selection criteria required by the MCO and highlights the provider's capability to meet the needs of the MCO's members. Before completing the application it is helpful to know

- The MCO's selection criteria
- The population to whom you will be providing services
- The types of disorders or illnesses that may be expected in that population
- The geographic area where the members are located

The MCO's network recruiter is a good source for some of the basic information about the MCO. Try to get answers to the following questions:

- Who is the employer and what is the business?
- Where is the business located?
- Are there several business locations?
- What types of health benefit plans are offered (HMO, PPO, and so on)?
- Is a description of the benefits for each plan available?
- What is the age range of members?
- Where do members live?
- Do members work different schedules?
- Is an Employee Assistance Program (EAP) offered?

Research whether there are any mental health or substance abuse problems associated with the industry represented by the MCO. For example, depression and posttraumatic stress disorder (PTSD) are common among the fire, police, and military populations; substance abuse is common in the auto manufacturing and banking industries, and eating disorders in white collar industries. Examples of resources for your research include the Communicable Disease Center (CDC), the National Institutes for Mental Health (NIMH), business industry health reports, and trade associations.

Before you begin to complete the application, review each section and make a list of the documents and information that are required to complete the application process. Clinicians' application requirements generally include

- Professional license number(s) and date of initial licensure
- Dates of graduation from undergraduate and professional schools and completion of internship, residency, and/or fellowship programs
- Liability insurance information for the past five years
- Names, addresses, and telephone numbers of professional references
- Faculty appointments and facility affiliations
- Completion of the confidential information section

Facility and program applications require

- Types of license
- Accreditation status
- Occupancy rates
- Average length of stay
- Inpatient and outpatient services
- Description of services or clinical profile
- Program affiliations
- Staffing ratios and the like
- Quality assurance program
- Statement of malpractice settlements or prior legal action

Supporting documents for clinicians may include

- Copies of license, board certification, diploma, facility privileging letters, liability facesheet, and DEA certificate (M.D. and D.O. only)
- Detailed explanation of malpractice claims (I suggest you provide a copy of case disposition letters)
- Current curriculum vitae, and so on

Facilities may be required to submit copies of

- Audited financial statements
- Published charges
- Description of programs
- Copy of license, accreditation certificate, liability facesheet
- Medical staff roster
- Malpractice claim history, and so forth

In addition to the documents required, consider other documents or information that add value to your application.

For Facilities

Submit a copy of your quality assurance and quality improvement plans, demonstrating your responsiveness to compliance with the managed care environment. If you have implemented any quality improvement programs with results that may be of specific interest to the MCO, submit a summary of the program and a summary of outcomes. Submit copies of certificates of appreciation; community recognition awards; outcome studies; and marketing materials, including program brochures, calendar of program activities, medical and professional staff continuing education programs, and so forth.

For Clinicians

Submit copies of seminar certificates that pertain to the needs of the MCO and its members, for example, a certificate of completion of a two-week course in brief therapy or certificate of attendance at a quality assurance program. Develop a profile of your practice, listing the major categories of disorders and issues (about four or five) and what percentage of your practice they comprise. List your treatment modalities. For example: practice is composed of 50 percent adolescents, 25 percent children, and 25 percent family; treatment disorders include physical and sexual abuse, eating disorders, attention deficit disorder, depression.

Also include a list of publications and presentations related to your specialties, and achievement and/or recognition awards.

Pay attention to the preparation of your application and supporting materials package. This is your opportunity to make your first marketing impression on the MCO. Incorporate the business skills and processes you use with other professionals. Prepare a cover letter that reflects your credentials, services, and desire to become a network provider.

Here is a sample letter:

Dear [MCO]:

Enclosed is my completed application, required supporting documents, and two (2) copies of the executed provider contract for consideration as an MCO network clinician to provide services to the City of Tulsa Department of Education.

I have been practicing as a licensed psychologist in Tulsa for twelve years. My practice is composed primarily of children and adolescents from ages eight to eighteen, with diagnoses of eating disorders, sexual abuse, depression, and attention deficit disorder. Family involvement is an essential part of my treatment modalities. I have two office locations, with day and evening office hours Monday through Friday and Saturday mornings. I have a twenty-four-hour answering service and am able to respond to emergencies within two hours of notification.

I have been a member of the Tulsa Board of Education Special Needs Project since 1988. We developed a program for teachers and school counselors to recognize eating disorders and sexual abuse in grades K–12. In addition to my professional training and experience,

I annually attend national seminars and continuing education programs. I am an adjunct professor in the Department of Psychology at
State University. Currently I am a participating provider with four
managed care organizations.

I welcome the opportunity to become a network provider with
[MCO]. If additional information is required please call me at (555)
666–7777 between 8:00 and 9:00 A.M., 1:00 to 2:00 P.M., or 5:00 to
6:00 P.M.

Sincerely,
Pat Advocat, Ph.D.

encls.: application, copies of credentials, contracts

One of the most effective ways to submit an application is to develop a checklist of items included with the application. This system informs the MCO that you
have included all the materials requested by them, and it shows you are well organized and able to highlight the credentials you believe reflect your ability to work
with managed care.

The two steps to the application process are (1) to make copies of the application, checklist, and cover letter for your files, and (2) to organize the packet:
first the application, then support documents in the order required by the application, and then additional documents and supporting materials. The signed
and dated contract is the last document. It is helpful to either clip the complete
packet and place the cover letter on top or place all the materials in a folder with
the cover letter on top of the folder. Insert the contents in a large envelope and
mail to the MCO.

One of the major delays in processing a provider's application comes when the
MCO has to request missing documentation or return incomplete applications submitted by providers. The time you spend preparing and completing your application will give you an advantage over other applicants. A well-organized application
facilitates review by the network developer and can lead to prompt submission of
your packet for review and approval by the credentialing committee.

A Sample Case Study

TCL Health Systems (TCL), located in Yuma, Arizona, is a hospital system providing comprehensive integrated behavioral healthcare services. TCL offers both
inpatient and outpatient mental health and substance abuse services for adults,
adolescents, and children. TCL has a twenty-bed adult, twenty-bed adolescent,
and fifteen-bed child acute care mental health unit; twenty-three-hour observa-
tion beds; eating and compulsive disorder, elder care, and partial hospital pro-

grams; detox unit and dual diagnosis unit; structured outpatient programs and aftercare; family, group, and individual outpatient therapy; support groups for abuse and PTSD; and a mobile crisis unit.

Behavioral Health MCO (BHMCO) is a regional behavioral health managed care organization managing the behavioral healthcare of 450,000 covered lives, including 250,000 commercial members, 75,000 CHAMPUS members, 65,000 Medicaid, and 70,000 Medicare members. BHMCO contracted to provide behavioral healthcare benefits to a defense contractor, also in Yuma, with 15,000 employees, 10,000 Medicaid members, and 25,000 CHAMPUS members.

BHMCO recruited TCL as the primary behavioral healthcare provider. The fee structures negotiated for the services provided by TCL follow.

Inpatient Services	*ComPro*	*Medicaid/CHAMPUS*
Inpatient units for mental health and detox (all inclusive per diem)		
Adults	$525	$500
Adolescents	525	500
Children	550	500
Inpatient chemical dependency unit (all inclusive per diem rates, including physician fees)		
Adults	$375	$350
Adolescents	375	350

Outpatient services	*ComPro*	*Medicaid/CHAMPUS*
Twenty-three-hour observation beds	$55 per hour	$55 per hour
Partial hospital program (maximum program rate $2,550)	75 per diem	75 per diem
Structured outpatient program (program rate; includes aftercare, lab, urine analysis)	2,500	2,500
Elder program—Medicare only	n/a	10 percent discount off Medicare fee schedule
Crisis mobile unit	n/a	10 percent discount off Medicare fee schedule

◆ ◆ ◆

Your participation in and success as a managed care provider depends upon whether you understand the components of the contracting process; know your responsibilities as a provider; and market your credentials, experience, and expertise. A final step in successful contract participation is to begin and maintain a collegial relationship with the provider relations and clinical case management staffs.

CHAPTER EIGHT

PROMOTING YOUR SERVICES

Aida Porras

Mental health practitioners frequently come to me, cautiously seeking marketing advice: "I want to grow my practice, but I want to do it ethically." This statement beckons thoughtful consideration. What is unethical about promoting yourself unless you misrepresent your services? Undeniably, the vast majority of clinicians received a clear message somewhere in their training that promoting yourself was not only unprofessional but close to hucksterism. Linda Lawless, M.A., a licensed professional counselor, wrote in an insightful article titled "Marketing Phobia?????":

> I have identified a new clinical syndrome specific to mental health professionals, Marketing Phobia. Marketing Phobia may be organic or learned. Consider our backgrounds. Mental Health professionals receive training to take care of others' needs, work in an industry that discourages dual relationships, and offer services that carry a social stigma (mental illness). . . . We can't tell people they need our services if we notice a problem (diagnosis in public), we can't offer services to happy clients' family or friends (dual relationship), and we have to be scrupulously honest in all our marketing efforts (ethical standards). Mental Health professionals have the makings of a real marketing challenge. Unlike others who sell products and services, [we] cannot offer guaranteed quick cures, reduced rates for frequent fliers, or speak about [our] latest success story in great detail.

The irony of this situation is that marketing requires good communication, active listening, assessment of needs, and recommendations based on those assessments. These are the same basic skills that are essential to the makings of a good clinician. Therefore, most mental health providers already have many of the skills needed to be successful in marketing their services.

Healthcare marketing relies heavily on the development and maintenance of ethical, professional relationships. Establishing rapport and gaining the trust of individuals or organizations are key factors that provide support for promotional activities. Engaging in high-pressure sales behavior is not a prerequisite for accomplishing your marketing goals. You must, however, believe in what you do. Your willingness to communicate honestly about the services you represent has a direct effect on what happens when opportunities cross your path.

The current managed care environment has dramatically changed the ways that you can do business, and promoting yourself is not only acceptable professional behavior but is becoming a requirement of maintaining a practice. When negotiating a contract to provide services to an MCO, insurance company, or other payer organization, you can ethically offer service commitments or guarantees (for example, free additional services if a substance-abusing patient relapses). When contracting, you can offer reduced rates for quantity referrals, and you should be actively promoting your treatment successes via outcome studies. All of this can be done without compromising patient confidentiality or professional practice standards.

In addition if you want to maintain any type of self-pay clientele or draw direct consumer referrals, you need to learn how to become comfortable with promoting yourself. Whether you work in a community mental health organization, MCO, or an employee assistance program, your skill at letting people know about what you do will have a significant impact on your success.

What Is Promotion?

The essence of promotion is educating your target customers about

- What you (and/or your organization) do
- When it is appropriate to use your services
- How to reach you
- How much your services are likely to cost
- What benefits or outcomes a potential client can expect as a result of using your services

Good promotion differentiates your services by explaining how you are unique and by identifying why you are a better choice than your competitors. For example, although you may provide the same general services as twenty other clinicians in your community, you promote yourself as the only provider who serves children, is bilingual, has evening or weekend hours, or makes house calls. In a crowded marketplace, it is important to establish unique advantages and notable points of difference from your competitors. This is called positioning, or establishing a market niche.

Our business environment is constantly changing. Therefore it is important to monitor your target audience's needs and their responses to your promotional activity. Maintain flexibility as you implement your plan. This enables you to change direction as the marketplace dictates.

There are many tools you can use as part of your promotional strategy. Consider utilizing a combination of techniques to reach consumers. Highlight your unique attributes as an individual or business entity by providing easy-to-understand information through your promotional efforts. You can make consumers aware of your services by planning strategic promotions to enhance your networking and referral development activities. Choose methods depending on your particular business development interests, your budget, and the time you are willing to invest in promoting yourself.

How to Position Your Business for Success

There is no single formula for successful positioning of your business. The key to devising a plan that works is knowing who your potential clients are, what they need, and where to look for them. Researching this information assists you in matching the benefits and features of your business to the needs of your target audiences. Your success hinges upon your ability to strategically navigate your business into a position where your prospective clients recognize it as the service of choice. Providing information tailored to their interests helps them understand how you can meet their needs while enhancing their perceptions of the value of what you have to offer.

To set up your promotional plan, you must first organize the information you have gathered about your potential clients and match it with your own. You can do this by creating a Potential Client Profile (Table 8.1). Utilizing each of the subheadings that follow, title a series of lists and categorize your information.

TABLE 8.1. POTENTIAL CLIENT PROFILE.

Sample plan: The overall objective is to generate referrals of adolescents, children, and their families to an outpatient group practice office.

POTENTIAL CLIENTS	CLIENT NEEDS	WHERE CLIENTS WILL LOOK FOR HELP	FEATURES AND BENEFITS TO CLIENTS	LIST OF CURRENT PROMOTIONAL ACTIVITIES	RATING
PARENTS OF CHILDREN AND ADOLESCENTS WITHIN A REASONABLE DISTANCE	1. Parenting skills education	1. Yellow Pages	FEATURES	1. Yellow Page ads in two books	6
PEDIATRICIANS	2. Convenient appointment times	2. Physicians	1. Twenty-four-hour emergency assessments	2. Ads in the *Chester County Gazette*	3
GENERAL PRACTITIONERS	3. Flexible payment plans	3. Schools/Day care	2. Community education classes	3. Attention deficit screenings four times per year	8
SCHOOL COUNSELORS	4. Referral resource for alternative services	4. Employee assistance professionals	3. Specialists in the treatment of children	4. Parenting classes	5
TEACHERS	5. Information about attention deficit disorder	5. Insurance cards and directories	4. Contract providers with managed care and county mental health agencies	5. Community lecture series	5
HOSPITALS	6. Information on acting-out behaviors	6. Mental health professionals		6. Regular column on parenting in the youth club newsletter	6
POLICE DEPARTMENT	7. Drug awareness information	7. Friends	BENEFITS	7. Networking luncheons	9
	8. Intervention for abuse issues	8. Hotlines	1. Easy access	Rating 1 (low) to 10 (high) level of response	
	9. Treatment by professionals who are trained to address the needs of this population	9. Newspaper	2. Convenient, affordable classes		
	10. Medication evaluation and management	10. Radio talk shows	3. Quality/Expertise		
	11. Support groups	11. Libraries	4. Payment covered by insurance plan or sliding scale		
	12. Information on parenting as a single person	12. Hospitals			
	13. Counseling				

NOTE: These are partial lists from a much larger report.

List Potential Customers by Market Segment

Develop lists of your current clients and those whom you would like to have as clients (Table 8.2). Categorize your lists by "market segment": the organizations that provide like services or the groups of individuals who require similar services. For example, your titles could include hospitals, MCOs, agencies, parenting groups. Your choice of market segments is influenced by your areas of specialty, services provided, and contractual relationships. When applicable, include age groups (for example, seniors or children), special issues (domestic abuse, divorce), or other specifics. Also include the names of any gatekeepers, such as employee assistance professionals and case managers, who could facilitate opportunities to help you get in touch with your clients.

List Your Client's Needs

Consider the types of services required by the client in each market segment (Table 8.3). What is currently being provided in the community? Are client needs underserved, or are there no services available? List all of your ideas and document information about potential competition. The needs of each market segment can vary significantly. Gathering this information helps you identify the benefits sought by your client, as you consider what you have to offer. Matching client needs to the benefits of your service provides you with content information for your promotional materials and helps you tailor promotional activities to alert potential clients about your services.

TABLE 8.2. POTENTIAL CLIENTS.

MEDICAL/CLINICAL	AGENCIES/PROGRAMS	GROUPS/CLUBS
Hospitals	Drug and alcohol diversion	Parents Without Partners
Private practitioners	Community mental health	Youth clubs
Primary care physicians	Libraries	Parent/Teacher associations
Psychiatrists	Day care centers	Support groups
Psychologists	Health and welfare	Community hotlines
Social workers		Church groups
Counselors		Business organizations
LEGAL/JUDICIAL	ACADEMIC	TREATMENT MANAGERS
Police	Universities/colleges	Employee assistance
Probation officers	Schools	professional
Judges		Managed care case
Attorneys	EMPLOYER SETTINGS	managers
Mediation specialists	Human resources	

TABLE 8.3. EXAMPLES OF CLIENT NEEDS.

- Convenient location
- Special expertise or familiarity with a problem area
- Quick response to inquiries
- Efficient assessment and reporting mechanisms
- Partnership with referring entity
- Good documentation
- Availability/convenient business hours
- Flexible payment arrangements
- Prevention/wellness services
- Excellent follow-up
- Friendly, helpful attitude
- A service that can anticipate needs and meet them

Where to Look for Clients

This list assists you in developing a focus for your networking and referral development activities. Where will your potential clients go to seek assistance? If you are seeking self-pay clients, it will be important to go where they go. Spas, day care centers, meetings of consumer groups, and community center classes are just a few of the places you may find them. Other clients seek out information in a variety of places: the telephone book, brochures, professional magazines, union directories, hotlines, or lectures. You may want to consider article or ad placement in these types of publications. It is important to note that when placing articles or ads in a particular publication, you must do so consistently over time. Rarely will a single article or ad yield significant results. There are exceptions, but the advertising rule of thumb is to repeat an advertisement seven times. This means it typically takes seven exposures of a message before a potential purchaser takes action.

In the managed care environment, the vast majority of referrals are generated through contractual relationships. Consumers often seek referral to a treatment provider by calling the number on their health insurance card. Therefore, it is important to be aware of the referral channels that are utilized by case managers and primary care physicians. Various plans differ. If you are a member of any MCOs, keep your profile information up to date with the provider relations department. Check all directories, both written and computerized, to be sure that your listing is correct and accessible to a potential client. Be aware of publication dates for other directories where you are listed, so that you can provide periodic updates.

Review your own client records to identify your recent referral sources and how the individual originally sought assistance. You probably know your key referral sources off the top of your head. In some cases, your ability to generate a referral from these sources may have changed. Changes in referral flow may indicate that it is time to adjust your promotional or marketing strategies. This requires further exploration on your part. The successful business owner is constantly monitoring these trends to determine where potential clients are going to seek help, what the agent of change is, and how to respond with a plan of action.

Describe Your Benefits and Features

As a consumer, we make choices every day based on the beliefs we have about certain products or services. Sometimes we make these decisions based on the recommendations of friends or colleagues. On many occasions, our decisions are influenced by what we recognize as the benefits we will receive by using a particular product or by the features of a service.

For example, a therapist whose evening hours were booked has added weekend hours. The feature is the addition of weekend hours. The benefits to the client are convenience, easy access, and a lack of disruption to his or her work schedule.

Why would someone choose you or your organization over another? Your statements about who you are and the services you represent can be a powerful motivating factor when a potential client or referral source has to make a choice. Be aware of the types of services currently available in your community, and be able to clearly differentiate yourself from your competitors.

You can develop a good description by identifying the desirable features your services have for consumers and then listing the benefits of those services (Table 8.4). Check with your current clients to see what drew them to your services as opposed to another's services. Satisfaction surveys can provide you with an ongoing report of how your services are being received and the benefits reported by clients (see Chapter Nine for an example of a customer satisfaction survey). Each target audience is attracted to several key features and benefits. Think of these benefits as solutions to problems or ways in which you potentially meet the needs of clients and referral sources. Write these down beside each market segment you are focusing on.

List Current Promotional Efforts

If you are currently engaged in promotional activities, make a list of the methods you are using. Rate their effectiveness from 1 to 10. You can get a general idea of your marketing success by reviewing the numbers of new referrals by month and relating them to your activities. Are you attracting the audience you targeted? Was your activity cost-effective? In other words, were you reimbursed for your

**TABLE 8.4. EXAMPLES OF FEATURES AND
BENEFITS TO THE CONSUMER.**

FEATURES	BENEFITS
Twenty-four-hour availability	Help anytime you need it
Multiple locations	Located close to home or work
Referral assistance	Choice of treatment options
Treatment continuum	Access to a full range of services with one call
Wellness program	Helps reduce stress and anxiety
Aftercare	Helps maintain treatment gains

expense and time? Don't be discouraged. Take a look at your new Potential Client Profile (Table 8.1). Your lists include important details about your target audiences and your business. Use this information to review your old strategies. Keep the activities that seemed to work for you, and use them as part of the new promotional plan you develop using the guides provided later in this chapter.

How to Promote Yourself

There are many options available to promote yourself and build your business. Developing a solid promotional plan helps you establish or increase your visibility in the community and increase credibility. Implementation of your plan provides the structure by which you educate potential clients and referral sources about the uniqueness of your services and the ways in which they can benefit from a relationship with you. It takes some experimentation and creativity on your part to determine the types of promotions that complement your particular business and personal style. As you gain experience in the area of promotions, you will find that some approaches are more effective and well-suited for accomplishing certain objectives than others. Review the examples given in Table 8.5 to identify which types of activities interest you. Develop a written plan for your activities. You may also want to consider developing some of the promotional support materials that are discussed in this chapter.

Developing a Brochure

A brochure is one of the most widely used promotional tools in business. When people call a business to ask for more information, it is the item they most often

TABLE 8.5. FORTY WAYS TO PROMOTE YOUR BUSINESS.

1. Write a press release
2. Put up a sign
3. Give a lecture
4. Volunteer
5. Do a health screening
6. Join a club
7. Donate promotional items
8. Get your event listed in the community section of the local paper
9. Give a media interview
10. Host an event
11. Set up a booth at a conference
12. Sponsor an event
13. Go to a conference or professional training
14. Call a potential referral source
15. Place a Yellow Pages listing
16. Write an article
17. Write a column in the newspaper
18. Get quoted
19. Send a newsletter
20. Send an announcement
21. Have an open house
22. Send out a brochure
23. Give someone your card
24. Place a display ad in the newspaper
25. Help a colleague meet someone they should know
26. Use your special event calendar as a stuffer when paying your local bills
27. Network on-line
28. Send a letter to the editor of the local paper
29. Establish a reciprocal relationship
30. Announce an event on a bulletin board
31. Do your own cable TV show
32. Offer to be a mentor for a colleague
33. Start a support group
34. Join a committee
35. Work on a project with a partner who can share the work and expenses
36. Get a listing in a professional or club directory
37. Teach a course at a local college
38. Place a classified ad in the newspaper
39. Offer an article by mail order
40. Write a note or card just to say hello to someone who regularly does business with you

request. A general assumption is that a business without a brochure is not really a business. For these reasons, the brochure you develop serves you by promoting a professional image, contributing to your credibility, and carrying information to the community about your services.

The information you choose to include in your brochure and promotional materials must attract the attention of your customer. The content of your brochure should match the benefits of your services to needs and interests of your chosen audience. Your audience is generally more interested in what the results will be (benefits), rather than how you provide the service (features). A brochure that offers a balance of both types of information is very effective. This may require you to develop specialized marketing materials for several market segments. Refer to your Potential Client Profile to clearly identify the needs of your target audiences and to determine the objectives of your brochure.

Before you start writing, consider what actions you would like the reader to take. They could be any of the following:

- Request more information about programs or services
- Call to schedule an appointment
- Consider a contact with you in the future (phone call, assessment)

The visual attractiveness of your brochure is an important factor. The type of paper, ink, layout (organization of printed material), design, and wording you choose all play a role by making a lasting impression. The size of your brochure is another thing to consider. Most brochures are printed on $8\frac{1}{2}$" × 11" paper folded into three panels or in half. Research the types of promotional materials used in your area by consulting with peers, gathering information through professional organizations, using a consultant, or reviewing the brochures used by your competitors. Examine them carefully to see how others describe their services. Collect the phrases that you find express some of the ideas you would like to relate to your customers. Take notes on the things you like about each brochure. What are the appealing aspects of the brochure in Figure 8.1?

Figure 8.1 is a mock-up of a folded brochure on card stock, describing the services of the Bright Family Center, a group practice with multiple sites. The overall brochure dimensions are $8\frac{1}{2}$" × 11". The headings are highlighted by the use of strong, bold capital letters. The copy has emphasis by using bulleted descriptions and deliberately separating key paragraphs. Here are some of the benefits the Bright Family Center displays in their brochure: twenty-four-hour access, seven days a week; a choice of treatment options; free community education seminars; family-oriented services.

Writing a Brochure

Use these general guidelines when writing your brochure:

- Keep it simple. A brochure that is too wordy will not be as effective.
- Use bulleted items to keep your reader on target.
- Use photographs only when they enhance the written description of your business or services. If you are marketing a facility, photos offer additional appeal. Not every brochure requires a photograph to be successful.
- A map is helpful, showing how to get to your office or listing multiple locations.
- Use charts or lists for a value-added effect. The reader can review all of your services at a glance.
- Offer a brief description of your services and how to access them.
- Include phone numbers and addresses in more than one easy-to-find place.
- Before you go to print, have your document reviewed by several coworkers to avoid typographical errors.

- Use the same paper stock, ink color, and logo (if you have one) in all of your marketing materials. This is also part of your identity. Reasonably priced color stationary and pre-formatted brochures can be obtained from paper warehouses, such as PaperDirect.
- Don't develop a brochure in a hurry. When you do, the potential is high for mistakes and disappointment.
- Get assistance from a consultant if you have no experience in putting a brochure together.

Remember that your brochure can be a pleasant reminder about who you are and what you do, long after your last contact with a customer. A well-targeted, professional-looking brochure can be one of your wisest promotional investments.

Using Direct Mail

Any mailing targeted to a particular audience is considered to be direct mail. These mailings are most often done in bulk and can include materials such as a brochure, a "Dear Colleague" letter, a flyer, or a newsletter. The purposes of these mailings are to create awareness, offer services, and generate a response or action.

The best reason to use direct mail is to keep your name or business in the minds of prospective customers after you have initiated a relationship. It should never be used as a substitute for personal, face-to-face contacts but rather as a supplemental strategy. Take time to plan your mailings by selecting the target audience you want to reach and creating a promotional piece targeted to spark their interest.

Your mailing list can comprise your own source lists (for example, sign-in lists from lectures, accumulated business cards, or roster of current clients) or lists that are available through direct-mail companies. You can find them under "mailing services" in your Yellow Pages. These companies often provide complete mail preparation, including folding, labeling, envelope stuffing, and metering.

All of these services can quickly add additional expense to your project. When working with a mailing house, get an itemized list of individual charges. Find out when the list was last updated and what percentage they guarantee will be deliverable. Some disreputable companies sell poor-quality, outdated lists, so research your selection carefully. Or if you are interested in purchasing an association list, be sure to find out exactly who the list includes. Many professional association lists include students or individuals not active in the profession. If you don't screen out these individuals ahead of time, you will waste a lot of time and money. Compare the prices of a number of list services before choosing one. Direct mailings done on your own can take lots of time. You should weigh the cost of your time against the cost of a service before deciding to do large mailings yourself.

FIGURE 8.1. BRIGHT FAMILY CENTER BROCHURE.

Caring for the heart of family matters

(610) 633-6353

Conveniently located

Bright Family Center has two convenient locations serving the suburbs of Philadelphia.

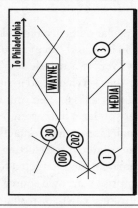

BRIGHT FAMILY CENTERS

WAYNE
2543 Conestoga Road, Ste. 203
Wayne, PA 19077 (610) 452-7555

MEDIA
Main Office
6565 N. Main Street
Media, PA 19074 (610) 633-6353

(610) 633-6353

We have a long-standing history

Bright Family Center has provided services to families in the community for over twenty years. During that time, we have demonstrated our commitment to providing high-quality treatment for children, adolescents, and their families. We offer many options to address the special needs of families.

Dedicated and experienced

Our medical and clinical staff are comprised of professionals who are board certified and specially trained to address family concerns and to ensure optimum care for all family members. Our professionals maintain staff privileges at local hospital and treatment facilities.

Community Service

Bright Family Center's professional staff are available to provide on-site training to meet the needs of employers, schools, local clubs, and organizations. Our speaker's bureau is available to provide workshops and seminars.

A warm, caring atmosphere is what you'll find when you come to Bright Family Center.

Raising a family is tough enough these days. When faced with a crisis or difficult family situation, it is reassuring to know that confidential, cost-effective help is available.

We provide a safe place to deal with complex issues

The Bright Family Center offers a comprehensive range of services. If you or your child is suffering from any of the following conditions you may need professional advice:

- ◆ Overwhelming anxiety or fear
- ◆ Depression and debilitating sadness
- ◆ Suicidal thoughts or behavior
- ◆ Threatening or destructive behavior
  - ◆ Out-of-control behavior
  - ◆ Substance abuse
  - ◆ Moodiness or mood swings

Without treatment, these problems may last for months or even a lifetime.

BRIGHT FAMILY CENTER
(610) 633-6355

Services include:

- ◆ 24-Hour Emergency Phone Line
- ◆ Psychiatric Referrals and Consultations for Adults, Adolescents, and Children
  - ◆ Individual Therapy
  - ◆ Marital Therapy
  - ◆ Family Therapy
  - ◆ Group Therapy

(Call for a list of our ongoing groups)

Assistance is a phone call away

When you call Bright Family Center, a mental health specialist will listen to your problem, answer your questions, and if needed, set up an appointment with one of our professionals. We will be happy to discuss financial considerations.

We also make referrals to local hospital programs, agencies, and other community resources. Call us if you need more information. (610) 633-6355

Professional Staff

Services will be provided by:

- ◆ Psychiatrists
- ◆ Psychologists
  - ◆ Clinical Social Workers
  - ◆ Master's Level Counselors

When you call to request services, our mental health specialists will help to determine which type of treatment provider will be right for you or your family member. All of our staff are specially trained to provide short-term therapy treatment, solve crisis situations, assess problems, and work with you to develop solutions.

Payment Arrangements

Bright Family Center is a member of many managed care networks. We also accept a variety of healthcare plans including Blue Cross, Champus, Medicare, and Medicaid.

Many plans require pre-authorization, co-payment, or referral from a physician. If you have questions about your particular policy requirements, please feel free to discuss your questions with our office manager. We accept Mastercard and Visa. In some cases, flexible payment plans are available.

The keys to successful direct mail campaigns are

- Targeting your mailings to a particular group that has a potential need or interest in your services
- Being prepared to respond to the results of your mailing with information and assistance

The average response to direct mail from audiences who are unfamiliar with your services is approximately one to two percent.

Planning is essential when using this method. In some areas, bulk mail can take as long as five to six weeks to arrive. (Don't forget to put yourself on the mailing list so you know when your direct-mail piece arrives). Check with your mailing house in advance to find out what the turnaround time will be for your order. Get the project completion date in writing. When you combine preparation and mail delivery time, you can see why a direct mailing is not a last-minute project.

Media Relations

You can promote any idea or story that you believe merits coverage by the press. For example, the opening of a new office, adding a partner, an upcoming lecture, or the addition of new services can be newsworthy if described effectively.

Publicity work can take on a variety of focuses:

- Generating media coverage by taking the initiative to provide media professionals with information and offering point-of-view pieces from your perspective
- Acting as a resource to the media by responding to requests for information
- Organizing event coverage and dissemination of information through media contacts

In order to contact the media, you need to compile an up-to-date list of the names, addresses, and telephone numbers of local media sources. Your goal is to establish a trusting relationship with media contacts. It requires patience and takes time to build rapport. If you take the initiative by generating ideas, presenting them in a professional manner, and staying in touch regularly with the media, your efforts will eventually pay off. A story in the newspaper or interview on the radio can increase your visibility and boost your credibility by presenting you as an expert to the public. The key to successful media coverage is to consistently highlight your uniqueness while offering newsworthy information to the consumer through media-related activities.

Developing a Media List

The focus of your list depends on your areas of interest and the location of your business. Consider every media source that might reach potential referral sources in your market segments. To get started with your list, visit your local library and review the directories that list publications or the names of media personnel. Don't be afraid to ask your reference librarian to assist you. Your list should include editors at newspapers and magazines, radio and television personnel, and professional publications such as clinical or association magazines and newsletters. Review the publications to gather a list of editors and columnists. Compile addresses and phone numbers of the publications. Local chambers of commerce, associations, and clubs may also be willing to sell their media lists to you. Add to your list as you find new sources. You should plan to update your list at least quarterly.

Developing a Publicity Kit

Once you know how to get in touch with the media, you have to introduce yourself. Your publicity kit is a valuable tool for this purpose and is useful in many other situations. If you are asked to speak to an organization or on television, the information that your hosts will be interested in should be contained in your kit.

The basic publicity kit can include

- A description of your business or services. This can be a brochure.
- A biographical profile. When writing this, assemble brief facts describing your accomplishments and educational background. Describe your relationship to the business or services you are promoting. Print the biographical profile on your letterhead.
- Copies of articles.
- A press release.
- A black-and-white glossy photograph of you.
- A list of questions that can be asked during an interview.

Place these items in a presentation folder to create a cost-effective promotional tool.

Keep several on hand at all times, and update them frequently.

Whenever you send your publicity kit to someone, always include a cover letter stating the reason for your correspondence and the results you hope to achieve.

Letters to the Media

If you have a desire to be interviewed by the media, write a column, or appear as an expert, you might want to consider writing a letter to a column editor. This tool is helpful when you want to contact the media with an idea but have nothing in particular to announce. When you present yourself or your company to the media, you need to provide some information that clearly sets you apart from others. Find out in advance which editor or newscaster would be most interested in your story, commentary, or article. Whenever possible use the individual's name and title to personalize your correspondence.

Here is a sample letter:

Dear Ms. Wordsworth,

The issue of violence affecting children has been highlighted throughout the media in recent weeks. Families and teachers of young children are experiencing difficulty in finding ways to address the concerns of these youngsters. Some children can experience fear and anxiety related to these concerns. It is important for families and teachers to be aware of significant changes in a child's regular routine—such as changes in eating, sleeping, ability to focus, and play—that may be the warning signs of unmanageable fear and anxiety. Please review the enclosed information about dealing with fear and anxiety in young children and consider a story or article to describe ways in which some families are getting help to address the problem of anxiety with their children.

I have been treating children, adolescents, and families in my private practice for over ten years. It has been my experience that children receiving early intervention have been able to improve their situation. Please call me if you have any questions. Thank you for your time and consideration.

Sincerely,

Justin Time, L.P.C.

Timing is a very important factor to consider when addressing the media. An effective strategy is to piggyback on current attention-getting news by sending a letter that identifies you as a local expert in that particular area. A letter of this sort could be sent following any kind of incident in a community that might cause anxiety in young children. A twist on the anxiety topic could deal with first-time preschoolers or kindergarten students. If your timing is right, the community will appreciate your comments and use them in real-life situations during a time of need. This is not ambulance chasing! The media searches out local experts all the time for commentary when such events occur, so there is nothing wrong with taking the initiative to volunteer your expertise.

If you are concerned about your writing abilities, there are places that offer "copy" that you can reproduce for your own purposes. Fred McTaggart, Ph.D., is co-owner of Healthwire, a company located in Kalamazoo, Michigan, offering mental-health, chemical-dependency, and general-medical topics ready to go. "The benefit to using a service like ours," he says, "is that the information is very detailed and provides up-to-date research for the general consumer or the professional. Providing this type of information to the consumer gives them something that they can take home and spend some time with." Using quotes from these types of sources or other references has a reinforcing effect on your comments and can enhance your query letters, press releases, and articles by providing additional information.

Press Releases

A press release is a document sent to an editor that announces an event, provides timely information, or issues a statement. Even if you've never written a press release before, here are some easy tips on how to look like a pro your first time out.

As you write the press release, realize that your goal is to get the reader's attention by provoking curiosity. All press releases generally utilize the same format. An eye-catching headline followed by additional details focusing on who, what, where, why, and how help the editor determine that your information is newsworthy. Include a quote from a key individual affiliated with your practice or organization who is involved in your announcement. If you are having difficulty thinking of a headline, look at the types of headlines that are used in the target publications to get some ideas.

The optimal size of a release is one page. Do not send press releases any longer than two pages. If you feel strongly that additional information is required, you may want to include summary information, such as graphs, charts, or fact sheets. When you attach additional pages, write the first few words of your headline at the top of the page and then the page number. At the bottom of these additional pages, write the word "more" below the end of the paragraph. Follow up with a phone call. Reiterate your story and recognize when you've said enough. Editors are driven by deadlines. Your awareness and responsiveness to their needs and deadlines help establish rapport, which can result in improved media relationships.

According to Donna Leaverton, community relations coordinator at MeadowWood Hospital in New Castle, Delaware, "You can never send too many releases. You may only get one media announcement for every five releases you send, but that one makes it worth your time." Ms. Leaverton adds: "Treat the media as your customer. Be available by responding quickly to inquiries. Provide a service by keeping editors informed. Direct your releases to individuals. Editors are more inclined to read something with their name on it."

Figure 8.2 is a typical press release, offered as an illustration of these tips and suggestions.

Publicity Photos

As you begin to promote your business, you can expect to get a request for a professional photograph. These photos, when done properly, can require two to three weeks for processing. Don't wait until the last minute, and don't cut corners for this expense. You *will* get what you pay for. Check with your colleagues who have had good experiences with photographers and get a name. Local advertising agencies listed in the phone book also can direct you to professional photographers who make their living taking head shots.

Your choice of clothing should reflect your professional image. Keep jewelry simple. Consider the use of a professional make-up artist and hair stylist. Usually the photographer can suggest the name of someone they've worked with before. (Ask to see pictures they've taken with and without makeup; it does make a difference, especially in black and white photos.)

Your photos should be black and white and should not involve a "soft-focus" process. If you are bothered by a few wrinkles, you can have those touched-up after the photo is taken. The printed size should be 5" × 7" or 8"× 10". When you receive your prints, attach an identifying label to the back of each photo before sending them out. An easy method of labeling is to attach a sticker with your name, address, and phone number, either preprinted or typed. Photographs can be included as part of your promotional or publicity packet, included with press releases, used in professional directories, included with articles written by you or about you, used in advertisements, or used in program guides for lectures.

Media Interviews

There are essentially three forums for an interview: television taped or live, radio taped or live, or personal interview for a written publication.

Regardless of your past experience with the media, you should prepare for all three types of interviews. This is your opportunity to provide the interviewer with useful information, which can lead to future opportunities for publicity. In most cases, you know the topic in advance and that gives you time to plan and practice.

When you arrive for a videotaped or televised interview, make sure that the

FIGURE 8.2. MEADOWWOOD HOSPITAL PRESS RELEASE.

Just above the first paragraph, on a separate line write release time. Immediate or for example, "FOR RELEASE, February 1, 1995."

In the right hand corner, place the name of a contact person and phone number where he or she can be reached.

Company letterhead

Clear, easy to read typeface.

Write the entire headline in captial letters and center on the first page.

Come up with a one-line statement or include a few words from your press release.

Write the body of your release immediately below the headline. Note the location and date of your event or announcement.

Use a quote from someone in your organization.

Double space with margins no less than 1 1/4" to allow for editing.

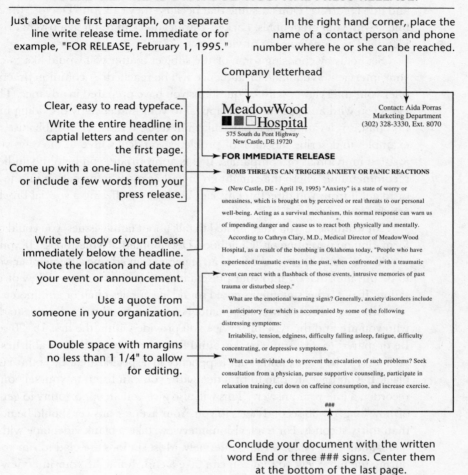

Conclude your document with the written word End or three ### signs. Center them at the bottom of the last page.

QUICK TIP: Include the WHO, WHAT, WHERE, WHEN, WHY, and HOW in your press release.

Source: Reprinted by permission of MeadowWood Hospital.

readout (the words that will appear under your image on the screen) of your name and title is correct. Don't assume that because they call you "Doctor" they are familiar with your credentials. Lack of clarification can result in a psychiatrist being identified as a psychologist or vice versa.

Set goals by choosing some of the subject matter you would like to cover in your interview. What kind of audience will be reached? A common practice is to offer your interviewer a list of questions you have prepared in advance. This provides you with an opportunity to appeal to your audience by providing information that is relevant to their particular interests. Whenever possible, use real-life examples to describe the kinds of problems you deal with and the ways you have assisted individuals or companies. If it is appropriate, you help the audience by recommending where they might go to gather more information on the subject or to get it from you directly. This can be done by offering a special brochure or article.

For example, if you were invited to talk about family issues, you could offer information on parenting or "Childhood Developmental Milestones." If your interview is live, you have to make these arrangements in advance. Remember, you have to tie this information into your presentation so there is a natural flow of conversation. If not, your statements could sound like a sales pitch or commercial.

Always practice answering potential questions in advance. Be able to describe who you are and the type of service you provide within the first 15–20 seconds. Be prepared to give some background for your answers that establishes you as an authority by highlighting your experience in a specific area. Be enthusiastic and brief. If you have no one to practice with, you can listen to yourself on a tape recorder. Time your answers. This will also give you an opportunity to get a sense of how long 15–30 seconds feels to you. Your average answer should be no longer than thirty seconds. For a television interview, take a blank videotape with you, a blank audiocassette for a radio interview. Most stations are glad to run your tape during the interview, so that you can take a copy home. If your interview will be appearing in written form, ask for a "tear sheet," an actual page from the publication where the article was printed.

As to specifics on how you act and speak during the interview, Table 8.6 offers some do's and don'ts.

Lectures and Workshops

If you enjoy public speaking or leading discussion groups, consider developing a presentation to promote your products or services. By putting yourself in front of an audience, you can prove your expertise, establish new relationships with customers, or enhance relations with current customers.

TABLE 8.6. THE GOLDEN RULES OF MEDIA INTERVIEWS.

DO'S	DON'TS
Always restate the question.	Don't feel that you must answer every question as is.
Use the interviewer's name.	Don't talk too long.
Speak with enthusiasm.	Don't go in unprepared.
Use good eye contact.	Don't turn your interview into a commercial.
Consider your audience.	Don't be too technical, unless your audience will
Be on time.	understand.
Remain positive.	Don't tell lengthy jokes.
Reframe negative questions.	Don't get emotional.
Clarify yourself.	Don't let your interviewer interpret what you say.
Illustrate your points.	
Spend no more than thirty to sixty seconds answering a question.	
Tell the truth.	
Be alert.	
Be aware of your body language.	

Before you get started, determine your goals for the outcome of this endeavor. Here are a few ideas:

- To establish yourself as a consultant
- To showcase your expertise so that customers will seek your products or services
- To provide your own forum for personal networking

Goals help you focus on the type of information that is of interest to your audience. These are some examples of solution-oriented topics for presentation:

- How to get over stage fright
- Conflict resolution
- Improving communications in relationships
- Managing anger
- Negotiating managed care contracts for group practices
- Understanding attention deficit disorder
- Parenting skills for the 90's

To find additional ideas for topics, review community education class listings offered through local colleges and community centers, and programs offered by your competitors. Consider direct requests for information from clients, colleagues, or other business professionals. Lecture topics can often be developed into training classes, or they can lead to opportunities for personal coaching.

More than ever before, mental health professionals are examining the way they do business. If you have an interest in utilizing your skills to be a consultant, consider developing programs to assist others by offering practice development topics.

Now it's your turn to think of some new topics. Remember to develop a program focusing on a topic or issues that allow you to demonstrate your genuine interest and enthusiasm about the subject.

If you have little experience with public speaking but would like to explore your ability in this area, join an organization that provides opportunities to test your skill and get feedback. Toastmasters is an excellent organization to join if you are seriously determined to work on your speaking skills. You can locate a Toastmaster meeting near you through the listing of special meetings in your local newspaper.

Networking

Networking provides opportunities for professional and personal gain that go beyond benefiting your current business. Many relationships that begin as networking result in new partnerships, job offers, friendships, and long-lasting business relationships. In the current marketplace, your ability to establish referral relationships is critical to your future success. Although it is time-consuming, networking is an inexpensive yet highly effective way of marketing and generating referrals for your business. Getting started won't be difficult if you follow some simple guidelines.

Develop Lists of Individual Names

You can get them from business cards you've collected, referrals from colleagues, brief interactions at meetings, directories, trade magazines, newsletters, published market data, or sign-in lists from lectures. Your list requires regular updates. Manage your list well and it will become one of the most powerful tools in your business.

Set Goals for Yourself

Determine how many contacts you want to make on a weekly basis. Decide what method you will use to contact them. Face-to-face meetings, phone calls, and letters, or combinations of all three, work well. Set up a written plan delineating your target audience, action plan, time line, goals, and any follow-up, just as you did for your other promotional activities. Find out as much as you can about each contact prior to beginning the networking process. Set aside time on a weekly basis to research new potential contacts, and to implement your plan. List your commitment in your schedule as you would any other appointments.

Develop Several Opening Statements

Having ready a clear statement of the reason you are calling or visiting, along with several statements of benefits, can go a long way in starting a conversation. Use descriptions of the benefits and features you've identified in your Potential Client Profile. Write your ideas down and practice them aloud. If you take the time to think about relevant information in advance, your confidence level increases because you will be well prepared.

Organize Your Promotional Material in Advance

Before you leave for the appointment, make sure that you have everything you need. Arrange your presentation folder or briefcase so that it is easily accessible. Bring information that may be of special interest to the customer. For example, if you are a provider working with a managed care company, it is important to provide information about your internal utilization review criteria and process, clinical program/service descriptions, information on how to access your services, and the names of key contacts in your organization. Whenever possible, bring a sample or visual aid, such as a chart that shows all of your services and locations at a glance. The chart provides an opportunity to ask specific questions.

Meet Your Prospective Referral Source

Use open-ended questions and active listening skills in order to determine the specific needs of the individual or group of people you are meeting with. As you encourage dialogue, help your customer(s) focus on your services by maintaining control of the meeting. Plan your discussion ahead of time, but be flexible. Respond to questions, but don't give out more information than they will need. This keeps the flow of information directed toward the interests and expressed needs of potential referral source(s). Your skill in this area keeps the people whom you contact from feeling that you are selling to them. What you are really doing is demonstrating customer service by offering information and assistance.

Develop Reciprocal Relationships

As you develop your networking expertise, you establish relationships with groups, individuals, facilities, or agencies who will refer to you. One of your goals should be to give referrals back to those professionals; a good reason you might do so is for continuity of care. More specifically, there will always be inquiries received in your office that would most appropriately be referred to another professional.

Making a referral is one of the highest compliments you can pay someone. You should consider giving referrals not just to those who refer but also to those with whom you would like to establish a reciprocal relationship. This type of relationship is often established when physicians and therapists or a variety of mental health professionals and hospitals work together. Besides benefiting your clients, these cooperative relationships can offer other opportunities. You might want to consider scheduling regular meeting times if you work with your referral source often. Find out how you can be of assistance to your source. If you take it upon yourself to help your referral sources meet people who would provide some benefit to their business, they will do the same for you. Invest your time wisely by developing these relationships. Over time you will notice the impact of your activities through referral patterns and through the relationship you have created by communicating regularly with your referral sources.

Record Your Efforts

Keep hard copies of correspondence in your files. In your records, document

- Date of first call, and results
- Goals relating to contact, and accomplishments
- Special interests and needs of the contact—as much information as you need to jog your memory for future contacts
- Notes that you take during telephone conversations
- Prioritization of your contacts on a quarterly basis

There are some wonderful contact management programs on the market. ACT (for PC and Mac) and SharkWare (for PC only) are very popular. These programs have the capacity to compile mailing lists, assist you in tracking your activity, generate reports, and do word processing, to name only a few of the features. If you have difficulty organizing your contacts, a management software program will offer some time-saving assistance.

Follow-Up

Once contacts have been made, you can never assume that your work is finished. Don't wait for people to call you back; take the initiative to follow up. Consider whether a call or visit will be more effective.

When making follow-up calls

- Be sensitive to time constraints. Check to see if you have called at a good time.
- Set up a list of discussion points to guide you through the conversation.
- Listen and respond.
- Be pleasant. Smile while you speak, and your voice will communicate appeal.

Your contacts need to be nurtured. This can be done by establishing goals linked to each name, with time lines for interactions to take place over a period of time. You can arrange your schedule on a quarterly basis. At the end of each three-month period, review your list and analyze the progress made. Did your networking develop a new relationship? Did it produce results? Which strategies worked better than others? It won't take long for you to identify those important contacts that represent your priority relationships. Those who are slower to respond should be monitored as well. Approximately 80 percent of your referrals will come from 20 percent of your contacts. Keep this in mind as you prioritize the contacts in your networking ventures. Seize every opportunity to meet people with enthusiasm, thank those who help you meet others, and remember that networking really does work.

How to Determine the Optimal
Promotional Mix for Your Business

Your decision about how much and what kind of promotional activity to use should be based on approximately two-thirds experience and one-third your perception of what you think will generate the best customer response. In other words, take your best guess. All of these directed efforts can be influenced by a good amount of luck. Luck is primarily timing. If you are lucky you will get a customer's undivided attention when you place an ad, get interviewed, or speak in public; if you are unlucky you will get no attention (the prospective client misses your mailing or ad because he or she is out of town the day it airs or arrives). This is another major justification for using multiple exposures when trying to communicate any message.

Experience is truly the best teacher, but most clinicians do not have a lot of experience promoting their groups or organizations. So this may be a good time to call in some outside expertise. Although a good advertising, public relations, or marketing consultant usually charges between $75 and $150 per hour, the cost of a few hours of advice far outweighs the thousands of dollars that can be lost through a poorly executed advertising or public relations campaign, brochure, Yellow Pages ad, or even one critical sales call.

Synergistic Marketing: The Most Powerful Tool

In the art of painting, rarely can the use of one color or tool create a memorable, in-depth image. Similarly, the most effective marketing efforts are those that combine a number of approaches building upon and amplifying one another.

The mixing of many "colors" or strategies can afford you the opportunity to combine more costly and less expensive marketing activities, stretch your budget, and get more results for less money. As you formulate your promotional plans, remember the Rule of Seven: It takes seven impressions before a potential customer can begin to evaluate whether or not he or she needs your services. In most cases, a fair number of tries is required just to get noticed for the first time. Seven impressions may mean seven TV ads; or, say, two newspaper ads, one flyer, one direct-mail piece, and one call from a friend. So use the combination of marketing activities that makes the best sense and suits your budget. Do make a commitment to be consistent over time because it takes repetition for promotions to work.

Notes

P. 123, *Marketing Phobia?????:* Lawless, L. (1995). Marketing phobia????? *The Advocate, 18*(5).
P. 133, *PaperDirect:* Their address is PaperDirect, 100 Plaza Drive, Secaucus, NJ 07094–3606. You can call 1–800-APAPERS for a catalogue.
P. 139, *According to Donna Leaverton:* personal communication.

CHAPTER NINE

CUSTOMER SERVICE

Ian B. Rosengarten

Everyone working in the behavioral healthcare industry has one thing in common: we serve people by addressing their emotional needs. Mental health practitioners have historically thought of the people they serve only as clients or patients, *not* as customers. For clinicians to change their perspective will take a shift in attitude toward recognizing that behavioral healthcare is similar to any other service-oriented business. As with other businesses, all mental health providers depend on insurance reimbursement or cash payment from clients in order to survive.

Clinicians working in all types of settings must understand that clients can and do go elsewhere if they are not satisfied with their treatment. Public agencies and government subsidized programs receive funds to care for the disabled or those on low incomes. Although historically, most of these clients could not readily access care in the private sector, this is changing as Medicaid comes under managed care. Soon this group also will have the choice to switch providers if they are dissatisfied. For any behavioral health service or product to be successful, one must listen to the customers and meet their needs. The bottom line is that behavioral healthcare is a business, and as with any business the key to ongoing success is belief in a *customer-first* mission.

The Value of Satisfying Customers

In a service-related enterprise there is one reason for being in business: to satisfy our customers. Whether the customers are clients, their families, and/or referral sources, they are the most important people we serve. They give us the purpose for our business. We are not doing them a favor by serving them; they are doing us a favor by giving us the opportunity. They bring us their wants and needs. It's our obligation to fulfill them.

By taking the time to know your customers and delivering what they ask for, success will come to your business ventures. Like the Buddhist concept of karma, customer service also transcends time. One good turn deserves another. For every positive customer-service seed you sow, you shall reap its rewards in the future.

Customer service can be looked at from two different viewpoints. The first is outward, toward your clients. As a clinician on the front line you need to provide insight, direction, and treatment that satisfies them. Secondly is an internal approach driven by a customer-first mission and philosophy that places customer service as the motivation for all that you do. This customer-first attitude needs to be instilled from the top of the organization down. Administrators or managers of mental health services need to support it by offering training and rewards for excellence in customer service.

Organizations, agencies, clinics, groups, and even small practices can retain more business if they:

- Support and reward excellent customer service at all levels and in all functions
- Promote a positive employee work environment

Employees and staff are your most valuable assets and must be treated that way. Creating, promoting, and maintaining a positive "service first" environment helps retain patients and coworkers. When good working conditions exist, customers report high levels of satisfaction and willingness to both continue treatment and refer others to you. In turn, staff who are given clear job expectations and are always treated fairly are going to create service excellence for your organization.

It's very simple. When organizations create a service-first work environment and use positive people management, external customers receive superior service and remain loyal.

Defining and Thinking Like Your Customers

Both internal and external customers define and derive satisfaction in their own unique ways. External customers interact with you on a time-limited basis, initiating contact from the outside. This differs from your coworkers and staff, whom we call internal customers.

Who are your external customers and what do they need? Different customer groups have their own particular wants and need. You never truly know those wants and needs unless you ask about them through informal conversations or by using more formal methods, such as focus groups, face-to-face interviews, and surveys. These methods are addressed in more detail later in this chapter.

Customer Service Needs

All customers deserve attentive treatment. They want fast and efficient service and caring, personal treatment. They need you to deliver what you promise with timely, fair resolution of complaints or problems. Most of all, they need to feel appreciated, so a sincere "please" and "thank you" works miracles.

What customers do *not* need is a lack of knowledge of your services, lack of empathy, lack of understanding, and poor personal habits, such as dress, grooming, and hygiene.

Most of all, they do not need a bad attitude!

The following are basic examples of what some external customers want and need.

Referral Sources. Referrals are crucial to your survival and consequently should be considered primary customers. Physicians, hospitals, and schools approach you for your knowledge and expertise; doctors, for example, want professionalism, consultation, prompt return of reports or evaluations, and an overall ease of working with you.

Individuals and Families. Individuals and their families typically seek you out for counseling or other psychological services. They want understanding, unconditional regard, respect, empathy, and consideration.

Payers and MCOs. Payers and managed care organizations authorize, monitor, and reimburse you for your clinical services on behalf of their customers, the employers. Payers want good communication, cost-effective care, easy access for clients, responsiveness, cooperation, prompt and accurate information, and a shared treatment philosophy.

Vendors. Vendors, such as billing, transcription, and testing services, help you operate more effectively and efficiently. They want respect, a cooperative working relationship, and, most importantly, timely payment.

Economics 101 Revisited

All business is driven by a variety of economic forces and assumptions. Supply and demand is one driving force that relates to any product and service. In the behavioral healthcare arena there is an abundant supply of providers, including such facilities as psychiatric hospitals and residential facilities, outpatient group practices, and solo practitioners. In this age of health care reform and an increase of capitated contracts via HMOs, the demand for providers continues to decrease. In this competitive environment, customer service becomes even more critical. Providing optimal service is the best way to gain new customers and maintain older, loyal ones.

Another basic business concept is the product/service life cycle. When a product or service first enters the marketplace, the most dollars are initially spent promoting it. Heavy advertising is often used to establish name recognition to position it and to attract new customers. If the services provided are valued, the business ultimately grows. As business expands, it eventually approaches a peak. At this point, a product or service reaches maturation as steady, repeat business continues but new business starts to decrease.

In order to avoid your organization's decline, the majority of marketing dollars now need to be spent on internal marketing, such as customer relations programs. It is critical that a business not become complacent when reaching its peak in the business cycle, which is all too easy to do. When more competition enters the marketplace, it is imperative that you emphasize maintaining long-standing business relationships. If you fail to do this, you will find your business sliding down the revenue curve and see a financial decline.

Justifying Your Services Via CQI

Over the past twenty years, there has been a growing movement toward using "total quality management" (TQM) and "continuous quality improvement" (CQI) in many U.S. industries. CQI has now also entered the behavioral healthcare arena. From psychiatric hospitals to small group practices, the tenet of systematic, process-oriented improvement is becoming a call to action.

Small organizations and group practices need not shy away from using some of the basic management ideas expounded in TQM literature. Even a group practice of five clinicians should have staff meetings where quality issues are discussed and actions taken. Customer satisfaction is one critical area that must be addressed in these meetings, especially in conjunction with how it directly impacts all staff. A CQI approach makes it easier to pursue external customers such as patients, referral sources, MCOs, and vendors.

Systems should be in place so that all customers, whether they be coworkers, patients, or referral sources, are able to voice problems or complaints. Follow-up procedures need to be taught to and implemented by staff. By promoting a customer-first mission in every facet of your organization, coworkers feel good about themselves and their jobs, and external customers feel the same.

Most organizations have traditionally exerted influence from the top down. Decisions were usually based on executive needs and communicated downward. CQI suggests inverting this management style so that staff and employees are considered first. Their input is now listened to and acted upon. Through this process staff learn to take ownership and invest in an organizational mission of quality improvement.

Psychiatric hospitals, residential facilities, and outpatient clinics are asking that clinicians and support staff alike look at the actual systems used and improve them, instead of focusing on identified problems that are merely symptoms of larger systematic failures.

For example, patient intake and admission systems appear to be fairly simple in a psychiatric hospital unit, but when we look closer we find that many people are involved, thorough data collection is rare, and paperwork is unwieldy. Unfortunately, when problems arise, such as a patient having a bad medication reaction, everyone points a finger at the other: the patient yells at the psychiatrist, she reprimands the nurse, the nurse blames the pharmacist, and the pharmacist confronts the admission counselor who forgot to ask the patient what medications he or she is allergic to.

With CQI, the whole admission process can be broken down into its minute details. Steps and procedures are mapped and charted by team members. Data is collected and analyzed. Recommendations are made, and eventually new, streamlined, efficient systems start operating.

Whether you are a small group of clinicians or you work in a large mental healthcare organization, accrediting organizations and MCOs are beginning to require outcome studies and other measures of quality. These may include measures of patient satisfaction, recidivism, length of stay, patient visits, morbidity, level of functioning, cost factors, work performance, and so forth. HMOs have made a major investment in creating "report cards," which evaluate services according to established benchmarks and standards. Soon these tools will be used to hold providers accountable.

Customer relations has an intrinsic place in these efforts at quality improvement. Successful strategies have many elements. Your goal is to build a CQI culture that identifies customer's needs, measures performance, and evaluates those needs regularly. In larger organizations, get middle managers and supervisors involved in the customer-first mission and focused on teamwork to improve quality. By serving as a role model for other staff, you can encourage them to reach higher levels of quality service.

How Can a Provider Differentiate Itself from Others Using the Customer-First Philosophy?

Here are a few ways you can stand out from the crowd in a highly competitive environment.

Competitive Pricing

Price is one way, although many clients are not price sensitive (because insurance often covers the costs of receiving care). The best way of differentiating yourself is in the excellent service you provide and its perceived customer value.

Employers are very price sensitive. They are demanding benefit plans that are less costly and more effective. That is why there has been a strong movement toward managed care plans, including HMOs and PPOs. At present, rates of reimbursement are usually a set flat rate (a case rate), a discounted fee-for-service, or a capitated arrangement. Regardless of the payment type, when negotiating rates with payers, you can use stellar reports of customer satisfaction and successful TQM systems as justification for maximizing your reimbursement rate within the acceptable range and for differentiating yourself from competitors.

Packaging

Packaging is the creative way you bundle services that are more saleable and palatable to the tastes of your targeted customer groups. For example, clinicians now package their group therapy experience and market it directly to behavioral managed care organizations. Here the value or benefit for the managed care company is primarily economic. After all, it costs them less to place eight clients in group therapy, facilitated by one therapist at $35 per client, as compared to providing individual therapy for the same clients at a cost of $60–$70 per hour. Another example: a therapist may use his or her expertise in attention deficit disorders by developing a time limited, psychoeducational class for a plan's enrollees. You can also package your customer satisfaction and TQM systems and use them to enhance your position in the marketplace. For example, one newly formed, large group practice included the word *outcome* in their name because of their emphasis on this area and their sophistication in outcomes compared to their competition. This definitely made them stand out from the crowd. Also include customer satisfaction and outcomes information in AMCD applications, and periodically attach these "success stories" to client reports. HMOs and other healthcare providers are beginning to report satisfaction levels and high ratings from accrediting organizations in their consumer advertising, press releases, and professional trade announcements. Why not follow suit?

Friendly First Contact

Prospective clients are now taking advantage of free phone or face-to-face consultations with therapists before making decisions about whom to begin treatment with. By offering this benefit, you break down access barriers to a client's first visit and have the opportunity to initiate the therapeutic relationship.

Value is in the eye of the beholder; many things that patients or clients value are intangible and/or subtle. These could be the courtesy and sensitivity of the staff; or a comfortable waiting room with extras, such as music, a box of tissues, materials, soft drinks, coffee, and so forth. Others may value a friendly receptionist, or simply not having to wait a long time to schedule a first appointment.

Location and Ease of Access

An easy-to-find location close to work or home, a transportation service, effortless access to public transportation, plenty of free parking, an in-house pharmacy, close proximity to medical buildings, office location on the first floor rather than upstairs, and so forth, are important to clients in general and especially to clients with mental and/or physical impairments.

Acceptability of Services

Overall satisfaction or acceptability of services is based on two factors. First is their *availability,* such as office hours in the evening or on weekends, walk-in emergency visits, and so forth.

The other is *accessibility,* which involves other elements associated with obvious or subtle barriers to care: perhaps having cultural, ethnic, and racial sensitivity, or bilingual capability. For example, having multilingual and multiracial staff makes a group practice much more attractive and accessible to both MCOs and clients. Other accessibility barriers are physical in nature, such as offices that don't readily accommodate the physically challenged. By becoming more available and accessible, you show your concern and sensitivity to your customers.

Promotion

Promotion of one's services through the use of advertising, public relations, referral development, and special events is resource intensive and takes considerable time and money. It is estimated that it costs five times more to find a new customer than to maintain an old one. Ironically, once promotional activities provide you with external clients, unless you have a customer-first mind-set and systems in place to handle the new clients you may lose them and waste limited resources.

Exploring External Customer Wants and Needs

How do we know what customers want or need? Simply ask them. Small groups or large organizations alike can accomplish much by regularly checking in with their customers. It is always important to know what you are doing right. More critical is knowing what you are doing wrong so you can quickly correct problems and improve service. A small investment in effort here will pay you back impressively with enhanced customer satisfaction and ongoing business.

Formal assessments can be done through structured, single-source interviews; focus groups; or administration of surveys. Each of these research methods has its particular pros and cons in regards to cost, time taken, and type of information you can gather.

Focus groups are recommended for larger organizations or businesses that may be considering entering the marketplace with new products or services. For example, a focus group may find out what kind of psychoeducational groups behavioral MCOs are interested in purchasing by including influencers and decision makers such as case managers, clinical coordinators, intake directors, and even executive directors.

Single-source interviews can be used by both individual practitioners and people in organizations as an excellent tool to get information on such diverse areas as the impact of new mental health legislation, trends in different needs for mental health treatments, or input on the viability of new products or services.

Here decision makers, key influentials, and power brokers are identified, approached, and interviewed face-to-face by using a questionnaire. Many times this is most convenient for respondents and can be conducted in the security and confidentiality of their own office.

Last is administering surveys. These can be done through mailing, over the phone, or in face-to-face interviews depending on your specific needs. Generally use the method that is most convenient for the population you are sampling. All surveys should be offered with the clear understanding that identities are held confidential, so respondents can answer candidly.

Regardless of which vehicle you choose, it is critical that you do something to learn about your customers—and more importantly, implement strategies based on what you learned. Never promise a solution, whether it is providing more timely reports, regularly scheduled communication, and so forth, unless you can fulfill that promise. An unfulfilled promise can destroy your credibility and is a negative experience you must avoid.

By definition, most people within the mental healthcare arena are excellent interviewers. Therapists in particular have all the necessary skills and training because they use them daily with their clients and coworkers. Be sure to use these skills with referral sources. When conducting a needs assessment, formulate questions that are relevant to each customer category you approach. Closed-ended questions that can be answered with yes, no, or with facts such as dates, numbers, and quantitative data are helpful, but they limit you in finding out what the customer is really thinking or feeling. So be sure to use open-ended questions as well, such as

What do you think about managed care?

How do you feel about the future of mental health?

What problems do you experience now?

How do you plan to address them?

Systems to Satisfy Your Customers

How do you know whether your customers are satisfied? Do you administer satisfaction surveys to individuals in all designated customer groups? What do you do with the results? Just like a needs assessment, customers should be approached, listened to, and responded to.

The best way to do this is by regularly administering satisfaction surveys, analyzing the results, and acting upon them—by telling your customers what you will do, and then doing it.

Surveys can be developed easily to fit your own particular needs. They are an excellent way to get feedback and input on many aspects of your services. Questions may address many variables associated with availability and accessibility of services, and overall levels of satisfaction. I recommend administering client satisfaction surveys on an ongoing basis and analyzing the results at least monthly. This gives you an opportunity to pass on commendations to deserving staff or personnel, and more important, a chance to address problems immediately.

A simple Patient Satisfaction Survey is found in the Appendix as Exhibit 9.1. (It is intended to be photocopied for your use.) Remember, generally the briefer and simpler the survey tool is, the higher the rate of response.

Never discount or diminish the importance of *any* respondent. For every person who mentions a problem there are at least five others who experience the same problem but never say anything; they just take their business elsewhere. Moreover, for every one who has a problem, something like six others will be told. Furthermore, just as in the kid's game "telephone," by the time the last person in the communication link hears about the problem, it has probably grown to catastrophic proportions. To illustrate, a patient complains of waiting an extra fifteen minutes for her appointment. Through "telephoning," this escalates into "My friend waited two hours before an inattentive receptionist told her, 'Dr. Smith won't be seeing you at all.'" As you can imagine, there are even worse scenarios than this.

What do you do with problems you identify? How do you nip them in the bud so they don't become cataclysmic? You confront them directly by calling or contacting the person who shared his or her negative experience! It is best if you ask clients if they would like to be contacted to discuss their problematic experience and obtain a phone number and convenient time to call. The individual who follows up regarding a clinical complaint should not be the individual's therapist. This will put the client on the defensive. Rather a supervisor should call and assure the person that you are concerned about the problem and want to learn more, so that you can respond. It's amazing how a direct, concerned approach can turn angry adversaries into loyal customers for years to come. So if a disgruntled patient says that whenever he calls he is always put on hold, then check it out, report back what you found, and tell him what you are going to do about it. Then do it.

In a clinic or group practice, it is imperative to monitor satisfaction levels of your clients or patients in this way. It is equally important to monitor referral sources such as managed care companies' satisfaction levels. Here the survey instruments differ but the process is the same:

1. Survey
2. Analyze
3. Respond quickly
4. Tell them what you are going to do
5. Do it
6. Show them what you did

Always complete this customer satisfaction communication loop to ensure that the person feels understood and worthy and that their need is being responded to in a timely manner.

Self-Assessment of Your Practice

I suggest that you take some time to evaluate just how user friendly your practice or workplace is for patients, referral sources, or patients' family members who call in for information. An excellent monitoring tool you can use is the "test call." Here you or someone you designate makes random calls on different days and at varied times into your clinic. The caller should have a formulated scenario of what she is going to say; this could be a request for information on specific services, or for general information (costs, methods of treatment used, etc.), or a crisis call. The test caller should have a Test Call Checklist (Exhibit 9.2, found in the Appendix; to be photocopied for your use) by the phone to document specifics of the call.

The Importance of Attitude

The following discussion relates to general working relationships with your associates, coworkers, vendors, and referral sources, including managed care organizations. I would *not* necessarily generalize this section to include your work with clients in which boundary and countertransference issues are of concern, both of which are clinical issues and beyond the scope and focus of this section.

A positive attitude is a state of mind that can be maintained through conscious effort. It is transmitted to others. The more you focus on positive factors in your environment, the easier it is to remain positive.

Your communication style should reflect enthusiasm and a positive attitude. Everyone relates and is more comfortable with individuals who are engaging, energetic, and humorous. Your communication style is extremely important when contacting customers, especially for the first time. Of particular importance is making a good first impression over the phone.

Actually, it only takes thirty seconds to formulate an impression of others over the phone. Thus your phone skills and those of your coworkers are important because 90 percent of the time the point of entry into your workplace is via the phone. It is critical that anyone answering the phone have excellent verbal and communication skills and techniques to ensure a good first impression. The phone must be answered promptly. All calls should be quickly routed to the appropriate party. No one should ever be kept on hold without having someone check back on the caller at regular, short intervals. (This is a point worth confirming on the Test Call Checklist, Exhibit 9.2 in the Appendix.)

Finally, body language is a vehicle that also reflects attitude. Body language is often the indicator that most influences our impression of others and their impression of us. Our bodies give clues in many ways as to how we are feeling. For example, just sitting up straight when you speak on the phone conveys a positive and self-confident attitude.

Create Long-Term Relationships

In order to succeed in the long run, you must invest time and energy now to reap the rewards of success in the future. Customer relations is not a one-shot deal. Long-term relationship building with new referral sources can be a long and arduous process. Physicians in particular are very difficult to develop working relationships with, mostly because of their time constraints. Fortunately, if you can do the little things they ask for that make their jobs easier, such as offering on-site services or submitting timely evaluations, your efforts will be repaid.

Developing and Implementing a Customer-First Work Environment

Aside from your external customers, it is your coworkers (paid or unpaid) who have the power and ability to make or break your agency or organization. Fellow clinicians, interns, and support staff control success and failure. Building a total service-oriented culture requires that everyone buy into a customer-first philosophy.

A harmonious work environment is a productive one. Whether you are loosely associated with other clinicians in a group practice or part of a larger, formal organization, every individual in it must work toward a common mission. When people are happy in their work and see their objective clearly, they reach for their highest potential. Any observer can tell when a work environment is untroubled by noticing people's attitudes; "free floating" laughter is generally an indicator of a good working situation.

Unfortunately, one person's negative attitude can turn a harmonious workplace sour. A dissatisfied person can act as a cancer in your workplace, spreading discomfort, disharmony, and dysfunction. Symptoms of this are readily apparent: poor morale, job dissatisfaction, turnover, abundant taking of sick time, disability claims, on-the-job injuries, wrongful-termination suits, dissatisfied external customers, decreased business, and eventual closure.

No organization, large or small, is immune to the wrath of worker dissatisfaction. Here I define *worker* to include anyone who represents you or your organization. A small group practice may only have one employee, possibly functioning as office manager, receptionist, and biller combined. An organization may also use a transcription service, answering service, temporary employees, and supervised interns. External customers see you and your organization as a reflection of all of these allied individuals working with you. That is why you need to have feedback on how they are relating to your external customers. If you don't, you may be in deep trouble and not even know it! Although you do have more authority and control over your own employees, even contracted workers, volunteers, and interns need to be measured by using the same employee customer-relations performance criteria.

Even if you are operating a practice and have only one employee, you are still required to comply with federal and state laws and regulations addressing equal opportunity employment, the Americans with Disabilities Act, and a multitude of fair labor laws. The following information is for your review and can be used if applicable to your specific work situation.

Hiring Practices

It is essential that every new employee, intern, and volunteer be given job-related customer-relations performance expectations and standards that are consistently adhered to and reinforced during the hiring, orientation, evaluation, disciplinary, and termination processes.

Without formal written policies and procedures established around these functions, you are setting yourself up for many problems, including wrongful-termination suits, workers' compensation, disability claims, and poor staff morale.

By establishing specific customer-relations criteria in your standardized employment interview form, you set the standards and requirements needed from the prospective employee:

- Does the interviewee have a positive attitude?
- Is he listening carefully to what you are saying?
- Is he enthusiastic?
- Is she polite (saying please and thank you)?
- Does she establish good eye contact?
- Is he dressed in professional, clean attire?
- Does she use effective verbal communication skills?
- Does he smile?

These are basic customer-relations attributes and skills needed for any prospective employee or staff person. Someone may have exemplary clinical or administrative skills but, because of a lack of the skills or attributes in the list above, be problematic and possibly destructive to your organization if hired.

Staff: Evaluation and Training

All staff should receive three-month, six-month, and annual evaluations of job performance in the first work year. Afterward, annual evaluations are appropriate. Again, evaluation forms should include the same customer-relations standards you have included in your interview forms and job descriptions. Without them you will not be able to assess or address potential worker problems.

Good customer-relations training for staff also has a positive impact on utilization rates, patient visits, and external-customer satisfaction. It is essential for you to educate staff about the importance of getting repeat business. Help staff understand this by providing a supportive environment and thorough training. The real key to is to get staff to think like external customers. Whether you are a large clinic, an agency, or a small group practice, the marketplace dictates that you provide friendly, responsive service to compete effectively and remain successful.

I've had clients tell me that they did not have enough funds for customer-relations training, that it wasn't important, or "With our staff turning over so quickly anyway, why invest the time?" What they do not see is the high cost of turnover in terms of rehiring, retraining, claims, suits, and so forth. What better way to decrease these costs—and more importantly build a strong group of contented workers—than by offering excellent training?

Disciplinary and Termination Practices

Sometimes workers become a liability to your organization. I have often witnessed people performing job duties well but failing in the area of customer relations. For example, a receptionist may be able to type a hundred words per minute with few errors, do billing, and keep schedules in an efficient manner. Unfortunately, her phone skills are atrocious! She always sounds irritated when answering the phone. You and other clinicians have heard her putting clients on hold, arguing, and ignoring new clients when they first visit the office.

Disciplining this person is not a problem if you have customer-relations performance criteria incorporated into her job description and have cited these in ongoing evaluations or disciplinary sessions. I suggest that whenever a plan for improvement is written, always have both parties sign it. Also make sure to schedule a time when the plan can be reviewed.

If you have followed established policies and procedures and have the paper trail to support them, you may terminate the employee without much fear of retribution. Because you have followed company procedures and offered the employee all avenues of improving, the reasons for the termination will be clear.

It also serves to defuse the emotional impact of the termination and relieves you from unwarranted guilt. If you haven't covered yourself and decide to let an individual go, be assured that the person's attorney will soon be calling.

Benefits of Having a Customer-Relations Committee

If you are a big enough organization, you can create a strong team effort through forming a customer-relations committee. The purpose of the committee is to brainstorm, formulate ideas, plan, and implement activities to enhance satisfaction levels of everyone who associates with your organization. Promote committee membership as being an honor. Give perks to deserving committee members by setting aside fun time away from work, possibly by having breakfast or lunch meetings. If possible, pick up the check; it will work wonders for morale.

A psychiatric outpatient department formed a guest relations committee that met monthly. Members represented nursing, social work, psychology, occupational therapy, recreation therapy, marketing, and clerical staff. Each meeting had an agenda; much of which was based on feedback from patient, employee, and physician satisfaction surveys. Members were held accountable to follow up with such activities as expanding the clinic's library, coordinating a monthly breakfast for attending psychiatric staff, or creating an internal newsletter.

Within six months they saw positive changes in satisfaction levels as reflected in the customer surveys. Patients said they were now being dealt with in a more caring and concerned way than before. Often they cited and commended exemplary employees to management. Employees regularly reported greater levels of job satisfaction. Staff turnover and sick days decreased. Physicians said that the clinic's multidisciplinary team was more cohesive and easier to work with than it had been. Because of this, the physicians became more available and accessible to staff and patients alike. Payers and MCOs expressed their impression that clinicians and clerical staff alike were more responsive and communicative.

There is no limit to what such a committee can accomplish.

◆ ◆ ◆

Here is a useful equation for maintaining positive customer relations.

$$IMPACT = ATTITUDE + EFFORT + WORK\ ENVIRONMENT$$

To have a positive impact on customer relations, you must address three major areas. The first is your own attitude and the attitude of all those you work with. A positive attitude always wins over the people you work with. Deadlines can be extended, mistakes made, and crises overcome if you have a positive outlook and face problems head-on. True, you can't survive on a positive attitude alone; there is a point where ongoing incompetence won't be tolerated. But occasional mistakes or problems will be accepted, provided you are liked by your customers.

Actually, many business relationships are based more on how you are liked than on competence and effectiveness. For example, a well-liked employee with average job skills will succeed where a disliked employee with above average skills may fail.

The second variable that should be considered is effort. When working, all of us give a certain amount of effort to our job. Although this may vary slightly, we usually work from an internal standard that we establish. This may be based on hours put in, productivity (number of clients seen), and so forth. To have a real impact on customer relations, you must exert a major effort. Going the extra mile means fitting in one more patient when you are tired, taking more time to explain a bill to a confused client, initiating conversation with someone in the hallway who appears lost, dealing with questions instead of deflecting them to others (who are just as busy as you!), and so on. A little extra effort is sure to be noticed and modeled by both your internal and external customers, thus establishing a better workplace.

The last area of positive impact on customer relations is your work environment. Here I mean the importance of having a clean, neat, organized, and cheerful workplace. A welcoming waiting room invites visitors to feel at home and be themselves and creates an expectation that treatment services will be equally caring and accepting. I recommend that you conduct monthly "walk through" audits, making note of areas that need improvement and then making sure the repairs are done in a timely fashion. By demonstrating that you are taking the time to do this, you convey just how important the physical work environment is to your organization.

Putting Your Customers First

I cannot emphasize enough the importance of your role in creating a positive customer-relations spirit at your place of work. *You* need to be a role model, change agent, teacher, doer, cheerleader, and quality control agent all in one! If you remember nothing else from this chapter on customer relations, let me suggest that you copy this summary and keep it close by as a quick refresher course. It tells it all as it really is!

The Customer Credo

- With no customers, you have no job.
- With fewer customers, you have less revenue.
- With more customers, you have more revenue and more opportunities.
- Customers: you need them more than they need you.
- Our customers

    Are the most important people we serve

    Are human beings with feelings like our own

    Deserve our most courteous and attentive treatment

    Do not *interrupt* our work—they are the *purpose* of it

    Bring us their needs; it is our job to fulfill them

    Do not depend on *us; we* depend on them

    Are our business

Note

P. 165, *The Customer Credo:* The author thanks EXSELL for use of the Customer Credo that closes this chapter. It is adapted from their video "The Unknown Sales Rep" (Copyright © 1987 by the EXSELL TEAM).

APPENDIX

EXHIBIT 3.1. BUSINESS LEADS FORM.

Company name: _____

Address: _____

Contact person: _____ Title: _____

Phone #: _____ Fax #: _____

Number of employees: _____

Company insured with: _____

_____

_____

Is there a contracted network?   Who: _____ Phone: _____

How are mental health benefits handled? Are they "carved out"? If yes, by whom?

_____

_____

Do they contract with an EAP?   If yes, whom? _____

Address: _____ Phone: _____

Contact person: _____

Role of EAP (consultant, assessment, counseling, referral, other): _____

_____

Are they local clinicians or out of town? _____

How are referrals made to the EAP? _____

_____

Do they see referrals in person or through a telephone contact? _____

How many sessions are allowed in the contract? _____

Are these sessions adequate to treat most problems? _____

What do you do with people who need more sessions? _____

_____

EXHIBIT 3.1. BUSINESS LEADS FORM, cont'd.

How do you (the EAP) choose who you refer to for ongoing care? _____

_____

_____

What types of mental health professionals are the hardest to find? _____

_____

_____

What do you require of clinicians treating your referrals? (Reports, follow-up phone calls, and so forth)

_____

_____

EXHIBIT 3.2. MANAGED CARE TRACKING FORM.

Company name: _____

Type of organization (Circle):   HMO   PPO   network   other: _____

Director of network development: _____

Address: _____

              _____

Phone #: _____   Fax #: _____

Review(s)/case manager(s):   1. _____

                               2. _____

                               3. _____

Organization information: (treatment philosophy; reputation; specialties they are looking for; geographic needs; number of lives they cover; how many providers do they have in a ten-mile radius; owned by; national/local)

_____

_____

_____

_____

Fee schedule: _____

_____

_____

Review policy: _____

_____

_____

Key employers they cover: _____

_____

EXHIBIT 3.3. PHYSICIAN REFERRAL FORM.

Physician name: _____   Specialty: _____

Address: _____   Office manager: _____

_____   Nurse: _____

Phone #: _____   Fax #: _____

Group practice or IPA affiliation (yes/no)   Whom: _____

How are referrals made? (doctor, nurse, office manager, and so forth) _____

Referral follow-up:

Date	Client name	Diagnosis	Physician contacted	Thank-you note	Progress note	Discharge note
____	____	____	____	____	____	____
____	____	____	____	____	____	____
____	____	____	____	____	____	____
____	____	____	____	____	____	____
____	____	____	____	____	____	____
____	____	____	____	____	____	____

Information sent: _____

Article title: _____

_____

EXHIBIT 4.1. NEW PRODUCT EVALUATION FORM.

On a scale of 1 to 10, with 10 being the highest, indicate how well this new service meets the following criteria.

Criteria	Rating	Weight

Financial Goals

- Meets/exceeds profit objectives

- Has excellent growth potential (demand for service will continue to increase)

- Will break even within six to eighteen months

- Has pricing flexibility

Criteria	Rating	Weight

Market Factors

- There are few direct competitors

- Services are not heavily regulated

- There are barriers to competitor entry

Criteria	Rating	Weight

Enhancement of Current Lines of Business

- Builds on current expertise and business base

- Strengthens competitive and market position

- Feeds other business segments

- Helps achieve company mission

EXHIBIT 5.1. THE CUSTOMER FORM.

Who Is My Customer?

Questions about the targeted group	*Answers about the targeted group*
Is the person who will be the eventual user (the *end user*) of your program or service the same person who shops for it (the *shopper*)?	Who is the end user?
	Who is the shopper?
Is the person who shops for the service (the *shopper*) the same person that the purchaser will seek out for expert advice (the *expert advisor*)?	Who is the expert advisor?
Who will be the final decision maker (the *decision maker*) on what will or can be bought?	Who is the decision maker?
Who actually pays for the service? The person who writes the check is the *guarantor*.	Who is the guarantor?

The Psychological Profile of the Customer

Does the same person fill each of the following roles? If not, what do the people in each of these roles *need, want,* and *value*?

• End user
• Shopper
• Expert advisor
• Decision maker
• Guarantor

Construct a psychological profile of each of these key customers by answering the questions that follow.

(Fill in a separate form for each kind of customer: the end user of your service, the shopper, the expert advisor, the decision maker, and the guarantor.)

What does the customer hope will happen if their needs are met? (The answers to this and the next question identify the customer's needs. This helps you define what should go into your product/service.)

EXHIBIT 5.1. THE CUSTOMER FORM, cont'd.

What does the customer fear will happen if their needs are not met? (The answer to this question will give you additional information about the sense of urgency of the client and information about their specific needs for service.)

Why are they shopping at this time? How urgent is their need? (You will find some customer segments, for example, the PPOs, who may not have a perceived urgent need. If you want their business, you will either have to be very persistent or create a sense of urgency with them.)

What have they been doing to meet this need until now? (This identifies the customer's perceived alternatives. These alternatives may be competitors. Or you may be able to partner with the competitors in a way that works for both of you and ends up generating referrals for you. In either case, you need to know who they are.)

Do they already have experience with your sort of service? Do they have a prior relationship with another provider of this service? (This identifies how much educating you have to do as part of your marketing the unique value of your service. It also identifies whether they have potential loyalty to another provider.)

If so, what have they valued and what have they wanted to change about the prior relationship(s)? (The answer to this question tells you what it will take for your service to attract these potential clients away from what they are now using.)

What do they see as the alternatives they can use to solve their needs?

What is their perception about you, your organization, and your service?

EXHIBIT 5.2. MARKETING AND SALES PLAN.

I.   Executive Overview
     The executive overview gives a capsule presentation of your marketing and
     sales strategy and plans for the next fiscal year.

II. Major Challenges Facing the Organization in the Coming Year
     A.   Competition

     B.   Strengths, weaknesses, opportunities, threats ("SWOT" analysis)

III. Review of Last Year's Marketing Efforts: What Worked, What Didn't, and Why

IV. Major Objectives and Directions the Organization Plans to Take in the
     Coming Year

     • Products
     • Pricing
     • Positioning
     • Sales operations

V.   Brief Description of New Products/Services and Product Updates (If You Can't
     Articulate It, You Can't Sell It)

VI. Sales Objective for the Next Fiscal Year; Strategies to Accomplish Objectives
     (Do a Few Things Well!)
     A.   Develop and close contracts with the following target groups:

EXHIBIT 5.2. MARKETING AND SALES PLAN, cont'd.

B. Target sales goal, by customer group for the next fiscal year

Targeted Groups for Next Fiscal Year	Number of Members/ Potential Clients	Estimated Sales Goal (Dollars)
State and County Government		
Business Coalitions		
Existing Customers		
EAPs		
Totals		

C. Major strategies to accomplish objective VI.A.:

VII. Sales Implementation Plan by Month or Quarter
A. Quantifiable sales goals (should be stretch goals but achievable)

B. Identifying prospective customers: prospecting

C. Promoting the practice (refer to Chapter Eight, "Promoting Your Services")

D. Advertising (list what you plan to do, by medium)

EXHIBIT 5.2. MARKETING AND SALES PLAN, cont'd.

E.   Sales materials (use sales collateral materials to reinforce positioning)

F.   Budget (develop a marketing budget, by activity, for example, the cost of traveling to conferences, and the cost of sales collaterals. Develop a sales budget—both the cost of personnel and the cost of operations.)

Marketing expenses.

Sales expenses.

EXHIBIT 5.3. THE QUALIFYING INTERVIEW FORM.

(Photocopy and use this form when you do telephone or on-site interviews.)

BASIC QUALIFYING QUESTIONS	ANSWERS
What is it that you need?	
Are you using any service to provide that need now?	
If so, what do you like about your current service?	
What would you like to be different?	
Is it likely that you will be changing your current arrangement in the foreseeable future?	
What would cause you to change your current arrangement?	
If you have never used this kind of service before, what have you done until now?	
How has it worked?	
What is causing you to look around at this time?	
How soon do you need this?	
How soon would you like it?	
What is the likely time frame for you to decide to purchase?	
Is there anything that could get in the way of your going ahead with a contract?	

EXHIBIT 5.3. THE QUALIFYING INTERVIEW FORM, cont'd.

BASIC QUALIFYING QUESTIONS	ANSWERS
Do you have a process that you go through to make a selection for this service?	
Can you describe the decision process: • The steps that are involved • The time frame for each step • Who is involved (names, and positions in both the organization and the decision process)	
For each person involved, what is their particular: • Interest • Responsibility • Title	
Who is the person who will have the final OK?	
Who is the person who will be paying for this?	
Is there anything else we should know in order to be able to address your issues most effectively?	

EXHIBIT 9.1. PATIENT SATISFACTION SURVEY.

To reach my goal of providing you with the highest quality care possible, I ask that you take a few minutes to evaluate my practice by filling out the *confidential* questionnaire below. I appreciate and value your opinions!

Mark the category (excellent, good, fair, poor) that most accurately reflects your evaluation of each statement. You may use the space provided on the back of the sheet for additional comments. Please return this form to the receptionist at my office at your convenience.

	excellent	good	fair	poor	not applicable
Is the office location convenient?	[ ]	[ ]	[ ]	[ ]	[ ]
Are the office hours convenient?	[ ]	[ ]	[ ]	[ ]	[ ]
Is the parking convenient?	[ ]	[ ]	[ ]	[ ]	[ ]
Is the reception area comfortable and clean?	[ ]	[ ]	[ ]	[ ]	[ ]
Is the office staff competent and knowledgeable?	[ ]	[ ]	[ ]	[ ]	[ ]
Is the nursing staff competent and knowledgeable?	[ ]	[ ]	[ ]	[ ]	[ ]
Are all staff members friendly, courteous, and caring?	[ ]	[ ]	[ ]	[ ]	[ ]
Are appointment procedures timely?	[ ]	[ ]	[ ]	[ ]	[ ]
Are office phone calls handled quickly and efficiently?	[ ]	[ ]	[ ]	[ ]	[ ]
Is the after–hours answering service courteous and prompt?	[ ]	[ ]	[ ]	[ ]	[ ]
Is your therapist friendly and courteous?	[ ]	[ ]	[ ]	[ ]	[ ]
Does he/she spend adequate time with you?	[ ]	[ ]	[ ]	[ ]	[ ]
Does he/she explain reasons for tests and modes of treatment?	[ ]	[ ]	[ ]	[ ]	[ ]
Do you feel comfortable questioning him/her?	[ ]	[ ]	[ ]	[ ]	[ ]
Do you feel he/she is knowledgeable and professional?	[ ]	[ ]	[ ]	[ ]	[ ]
Do you think our fees are fair and reasonable?	[ ]	[ ]	[ ]	[ ]	[ ]
Has your billing been accurate, efficient, and timely?	[ ]	[ ]	[ ]	[ ]	[ ]
Do you receive adequate help with your insurance claims?	[ ]	[ ]	[ ]	[ ]	[ ]

THANK YOU

EXHIBIT 9.2. TEST CALL CHECKLIST.

Caller: _____ Date: _____ Time: _____

	Person answering call	# rings	# seconds on hold	identified self
1.	_____	_____	_____	_____
2.	_____	_____	_____	_____
3.	_____	_____	_____	_____

The following data was gathered

	yes	no
1. Name of caller	[ ]	[ ]
2. Name of referral source	[ ]	[ ]
3. Address of caller	[ ]	[ ]
4. Problem of caller	[ ]	[ ]

Benefits explained

	yes	no
1. Based on problem, benefits of organization explained	[ ]	[ ]

Plan of Action

	yes	no
1. Person should come for an appointment	[ ]	[ ]
2. Appointment set	[ ]	[ ]
3. Directions given	[ ]	[ ]
4. Referred to other resource	[ ]	[ ]

Phone behavior of person taking call

Circle one of the following, from 1 to 5

1. Disorganized	1 2 3 4 5	Organized
2. Discourteous	1 2 3 4 5	Courteous
3. Nonassertive	1 2 3 4 5	Assertive
4. Nonprofessional	1 2 3 4 5	Professional
5. Nondirect	1 2 3 4 5	Goal-directed
6. No action plan given	1 2 3 4 5	Plan of action given
7. Inaccurate information given	1 2 3 4 5	Accurate information given

ABOUT THE AUTHORS

David W. Allen, Jr., is a healthcare consulting principal with the Minneapolis office of McGladrey & Pullen. Allen provides strategic, management, and operational consultation services to healthcare organizations across the country. His seventeen years of health care management experience include senior management positions with a major national managed care company, two healthcare provider organizations, and six years as a consultant. Over a period of seven years with the Prudential Health Care Plans, the HMO subsidiary of the Prudential Insurance Company, he was on the management staff at corporate headquarters in Newark, the assistant comptroller of PruCare of Houston, director of administration of PruCare of Illinois, and vice president of PruCare of Oklahoma City. He also served as executive director of the Central Oklahoma Medical Group, a forty-physician multispecialty group practice in Oklahoma City. Finally, he served as executive director of Psychiatric Services of Houston, a multidisciplinary behavioral health delivery system.

A full-time consultant since 1989, Allen has worked with a wide variety of healthcare organizations. He holds a degree in economics from the Wharton School at the University of Pennsylvania.

Jeri Davis is recognized as one of the founders of the behavioral healthcare marketing field. Since the early 1980s, she has designed marketing systems and methods that have been implemented nationwide by the largest behavioral health delivery systems in the country. In her roles as the director of marketing for Charter Medical Corporation and the first vice president of marketing for National Medical Specialty Hospital Group, she trained hundreds of clinicians, professional marketers, and healthcare managers in both basic and sophisticated business development techniques.

In 1989, Davis established a national consulting firm specializing in helping clinical professionals understand and respond to the changing managed care environment. Her clients include large behavioral health provider groups, psychiatric and medical/surgical hospital-based delivery systems, state departments of mental health, community mental health centers, national associations, and managed behavioral healthcare organizations. She assists these delivery systems with strategic planning, recruitment, managed care relationship building, and marketing systems development and implementation.

Davis is the national managed care consultant for the American Mental Health Counselors Association and is a frequent speaker for the Institute for Behavioral Healthcare, the National Community Mental Healthcare Council, the National Association of Psychiatric Health Care Systems, and the American Hospital Association, Section for Psychiatric and Substance Abuse.

Davis holds an M.B.A. from the University of South Florida, where she also completed Ph.D. course work in clinical psychology.

Michael A. Freeman, M.D., is the chairman of the **Behavioral Healthcare *Tomorrow*** national dialogue conference, the editor-in-chief of the *Behavioral Healthcare* Tomorrow journal, and the general editor of the Jossey-Bass Managed Behavioral Healthcare Library. He also serves as the CEO of the Partnership for Behavioral Healthcare and the president of the Institute for Behavioral Healthcare; both organizations are dedicated to improving American and global mental health and addiction treatment benefits, management, services, and outcomes.

Dr. Freeman is a psychiatrist and a member of the clinical faculty at the Langley Porter Psychiatric Institute of the University of California, San Francisco, Medical Center. He is a specialist and consultant in the managed behavioral healthcare purchasing, managed care, and services fields.

Bruce C. Gorman is a vice president, public sector programs for Medco Behavioral Care Corporation (MBC). In this position, he serves as a senior corporate authority on provider organization relations, healthcare delivery systems, private/public integration issues, and new program development issues, particularly for those programs which involve multiple delivery systems and complex, large-scale benefits management. Previously, he was responsible for American Biodyne, Inc.'s (ABI)

Network Development and Contracting Division. He joined American Biodyne, now part of MBC, in 1989, from his position as administrator for the Aetna Life Insurance Company. While at Aetna, he developed and managed Aetna-sponsored managed care systems throughout the western United States and was responsible for oversight of their largest managed care operation, located in California. He has spent eighteen years in the healthcare management field, serving in a variety of operations, development, and marketing capacities. He also is a well-known author and lecturer in the fields of managed care, provider business development, and health economics. He holds a master's degree in city and regional planning from Rutgers University and graduated cum laude with a B.S. in economics from the University of Maryland.

Nancy Lucinian is the marketing director and director of managed care for Cedar Vista Psychiatric Services, a full-service psychiatric facility located in Fresno, California, where she is responsible for strategic planning, product promotion, and managed care contracting.

Lucinian has fourteen years of healthcare marketing experience, working primarily with behavioral healthcare programs. Her expertise includes successfully marketing her own private practice. She made the switch to hospital marketing, combining her skills as a clinician with her marketing expertise as the marketing/assessment specialist for Community Hospitals of Central California. She was promoted to the marketing department as hospital marketing liaison. For the last eight years she has served in a senior management position as director of marketing/managed care. She also acts as a consultant to clinicians in the development of their clinical practice, focusing on marketing and managed care issues and strategies. Prior to her affiliation with Cedar Vista, she successfully marketed and promoted a chemical dependency program for adolescents.

Lucinian holds a master's degree in social work from California State University, Fresno, and a bachelor's degree in psychology from California State University, Hayward.

Dee Pearce has more than twenty years' experience in healthcare management and as a consultant to senior healthcare executives. She began her healthcare career as a department manager in an inpatient setting for patients in psychiatry and physical medicine. She has been both a clinical and a classroom instructor, teaching and lecturing at San Jose State University, San Francisco State University, and California State University, Hayward, as well as managing clinical interns. During this period she served for four years on the Contra Costa County (California) mental health advisory board and for two years chaired the board.

In 1990 Pearce was recruited to MECON, Inc., a national healthcare operations improvement consulting and software company, as vice president for business development. For the past year she has been a senior consultant for the Permanente Medical Group of the managed care giant Kaiser Permanente of Northern California.

Pearce has published articles in a number of healthcare journals. At the University of California, Berkeley, a women's fraternal organization has created and annually awards the Dee Pearce leadership award to an undergraduate woman.

Aida Porras is director of marketing and managed care contracting for Meadow-Wood Behavioral Health System, an integrated network with locations in Delaware and Pennsylvania. She has been an active leader in the organization's pursuit of creative contracting ventures and affiliations. She is a licensed marriage family child counselor (MFCC) who specializes in the treatment of victims. She is currently a volunteer for a domestic abuse shelter in Pennsylvania. She is a board member of the Women's Theater Ensemble in Philadelphia, where her writing on domestic abuse was recently performed.

Ian B. Rosengarten is the president of I.B.R. and Associates, a marketing and management firm based in La Jolla, California. His marketing and management expertise lies primarily within the behavioral healthcare arena, where he has spent the last twenty years of his career. Prior to doing consulting work, he was director of marketing for Alvarado Parkway Institute, a psychiatric and chemical dependency hospital in San Diego, California. He has also served as a program director for behavioral health services for Horizon Mental Health Services, Inc. His experience in service/product development, contract administration, management, planning, customer relations, and communication laid the foundation for his present consulting business. He has also trained professionals nationally. He is the author of *The Mental Health Practitioner's Primer* and *How to Market Your Business* and has published articles in many trade journals.

Rosengarten received his master's degree in counseling from St. Michael's College and his master's of public health in health service administration from San Diego State University.

Helen A. White is a cofounder of MTC and the senior vice president for managed care. MTC is a healthcare consulting firm that offers a broad base of administrative and technical support services in strategic planning, managed care, information and management systems development, and materials management. She is an executive with more than twenty years in healthcare management and consultation. In addition to her extensive and progressive management skills, White's experience includes business development and operations management, managed care, marketing strategies for education and services, international recruitment, strategic planning, and healthcare network development. Prior to joining MTC, she was the founder and president of an international professional recruitment firm and the vice president for patient care services in two acute care facilities.

White received her bachelor of science in education from Washington Technical Institute, a master's in liberal science (MLS) in humanities from Georgetown University, and a master's in business administration in healthcare finance from Marymount University. She has developed and presented courses ranging from credentialing and network management to the administration and management of major capital assets in healthcare at the college level as well as for local, national, and international seminars. She is currently an adjunct professor at Averet.

INDEX